Learning Democracy in School and Society

Learning Democracy in School and Society

Education, Lifelong Learning, and the Politics of Citizenship

Gert J.J. Biesta
University of Stirling, UK

SENSE PUBLISHERS
ROTTERDAM/BOSTON/TAIPEI

A C.I.P. record for this book is available from the Library of Congress.

ISBN: 978-94-6091-510-9 (paperback)
ISBN: 978-94-6091-511-6 (hardback)
ISBN: 978-94-6091-512-3 (e-book)

Published by: Sense Publishers,
P.O. Box 21858,
3001 AW Rotterdam,
The Netherlands
https://www.sensepublishers.com

Printed on acid-free paper

TABLE OF CONTENTS

ACKNOWLEDGEMENTS

The ideas presented in this book are based on work I have done over the past decade on the relationships between education, lifelong learning, citizenship and democracy. The book focuses mainly on theoretical and policy dimensions. Empirical research which has been informed by these ideas and which, in turn, has informed the development of these ideas has been published elsewhere. The chapters in this book are informed by work that has been published before, but have been thoroughly revised for the purpose of this publication. As with all writing, this book is the outcome of many conversations and discussions I have had with friends and colleagues around the world, and is also strongly informed by conference presentations, seminars and courses I have given on these topics and on the input from many of those who have attended them. I am very grateful for these interactions. I would particularly like to thank Robert Lawy, Claudia Ruitenberg, Tyson Lewis, Maarten Simons, Mark Priestley and Charles Bingham for providing me with opportunities for developing my ideas and for constructive feedback on my work. I have also benefited tremendously from visiting professorships at Örebro University and Mälardalen University, Sweden, and would like to thank Tomas Englund and Carl Anders Säfström for making this possible and for many fruitful conversations. I would also like to thank Peter de Liefde for his support and his willingness to publish this book.

Stirling, November 2010.

Prologue

Learning Democracy in School and Society

Policy makers and politicians often see education as a key instrument for the 'production' of good citizens. This can not only be seen in the fact that over the past decades much has been invested in the development and improvement of citizenship education in schools, colleges and universities. It is also that when something appears to be wrong with citizenship – when there is low voter turn-out, when opinion polls show a declining interest in politics, or when there is an increase in so-called anti-social behaviour – politicians often tend to point the finger at education, arguing that parents are failing to raise their children properly and that schools are not doing enough in teaching the citizens of the future. The problem with this way of thinking is that it puts too much emphasis on the teaching of citizenship and gives too little consideration to the ways in which citizenship is actually learned in and through the processes and practices that make up the everyday lives of children, young people and adults.

While teaching definitely has a role to play, it is far from the only factor that matters in the ongoing formation of democratic citizens. The potential impact of citizenship teaching is always mediated by what children and young people experience in their everyday lives about democratic ways of acting and being and about their own position as citizens – and such everyday 'lessons' in citizenship are not necessarily always sending out positive messages. The responsibility for citizenship learning and, through this, for the quality of democratic life more generally, therefore cannot be confined to families, schools, colleges and universities, but has to be seen as a responsibility of society as a whole. This points the finger straight back at policy makers and politicians, as their decisions have a crucial impact on the conditions that shape the everyday lives of children, young people and adults and thus on the conditions under which citizenship is enacted and learned.

In this book I look at the relationships between education, lifelong learning and democratic citizenship from this wider angle, emphasising the importance of the democratic quality of the processes and practices that make up the everyday lives of children, young people and adults for their ongoing formation as democratic citizens. I focus, in other words, on the ways in which democracy is learned in school and in society. In the seven chapters that follow I combine theoretical and historical work with critical analysis of policies and wider developments in the field of citizenship education and civic learning, in order to highlight the particular notions of citizenship and democracy that are being promoted and the particular expectations about learning and education that are being pursued. I do this across a number of different educational domains – including schools, higher education, adult education and lifelong learning – and with regard to a number of different geographical locations, ranging from the Scottish Curriculum for Excellence and the English framework for citizenship education to European higher education policy and research, and national and international developments in the field of adult education and lifelong learning.

My overall ambition with this book is to urge educators, educationalists, policy makers and politicians to move beyond an exclusive focus on the teaching of citizenship towards an outlook that acknowledges the learning that goes on in school and society. This is not only important in order to understand the complexities of such learning, but can also help to formulate more precise and more realistic expectations about what schools and other educational institutions can actually achieve. It can also help to highlight the particular responsibilities of other parties in the promotion of democratic citizenship and the improvement of democratic life more generally.

The line of thinking I put forward through the chapters in this book responds to a number of trends in the field. Against the idea that citizenship is first and foremost a matter of *individuals* and their knowledge, skills, dispositions and individual responsibilities, I argue for the need to focus on individuals-in-interaction and individuals-in-context and on the crucial role that people's 'actual condition of citizenship' plays in the ways in which they learn and enact their democratic citizenship. Against the trend to see the domain of citizenship first and foremost in *social* terms, that is, in terms of 'good,' socially adaptive and integrative behaviour, I argue for the need to keep the question of citizenship focused on democracy and democratic politics. This means that citizenship has first of all to do with questions of political engagement and collective decision making and with actions in the public sphere which focus on the translation of private issues into collective concerns. Citizenship thus involves more than only doing good work in the local community but requires an ongoing orientation towards the wider political values of justice, equality and freedom. Against the trend to connect citizenship first and foremost to *communities of sameness*, I highlight the importance of plurality and difference in understanding and enacting democratic citizenship. And against the trend to see the role of learning and education first and foremost in *functional* terms – focusing on how the existing socio-political order can be reproduced and how 'newcomers' can be included in this order – I highlight the importance of processes and practices that challenge the status quo in the name of democracy and democratisation.

The theoretical 'device' I employ throughout this book is the distinction between what I refer to as a *socialisation* conception of civic learning and citizenship education and a *subjectification* conception of civic learning and citizenship education. Whereas the first focuses on the role of learning and education in the reproduction of the existing socio-political order and thus on the adjustment of individuals to the existing order, the second has an orientation towards the promotion of political agency and democratic subjectivity, highlighting that democratic citizenship is not simply an existing identity that individuals just need to adopt, but is an ongoing process that is fundamentally open towards the future.

From this emerges a view of democracy as an ongoing collective experiment. Following Ranson (1998, p. 9) I refer to this experiment as the 'learning democracy.'

I do this not only in order to highlight that a reflective engagement with the experiment of democracy requires that we learn from, in and through our engagement with it. I also use the phrase as a reminder of the democratic potential of the wider idea of the learning society and as a warning against the tendency to reduce the learning society to a 'learning economy' in which questions about learning are predominantly driven by economic imperatives. While I do wish to emphasise that learning can make an important contribution to democracy and democratisation, it is important not to forget that learning can only do so much. I say this because there is a growing tendency in contemporary politics to reformulate policy issues into learning problems and thus leave it to individuals and their learning to solve problems that actually should be solved at a collective level, through structural change and government action. The rise of a strictly economic interpretation of lifelong learning which demands from individuals that they keep upgrading their skills and qualifications in order to remain employable, is an example of the workings of a 'politics of learning' in which structural issues concerning the global labour market are entirely addressed in terms of individuals and their learning. This should serve as a reminder that the question of democracy and democratic citizenship cannot be *solved* through learning but also requires attention to structural and infrastructural aspects, including the resources for and material and social conditions of people's citizenship.

The book is organised in the following way. In chapter 1 – *From Teaching Citizenship to Learning Democracy* – I set out my case for a shift in attention from the teaching of citizenship to the learning of democracy and to the conditions under which such learning takes place. I discuss the recent history of thinking about citizenship and citizenship education, focusing on developments in Britain. Against this background I identify some of the limitations in current thinking about citizenship education and argue for a more situated and contextualised approach. Chapter 2 – *Curriculum, Citizenship and Democracy* – focuses on the role of citizenship in the Scottish National Curriculum called 'Curriculum for Excellence.' I identify and characterise the main trends in the Scottish approach and discuss some of the problems with the idea of 'responsible citizenship' as articulated in curriculum documents and policies. In chapter 3 – *European Citizenship and Higher Education* – I turn to recent developments at the European level. I analyse the ideas about citizenship and democracy that are being promoted, particularly in relation to European higher education, and raise questions about the limitations of these ideas. Chapter 4 – *Knowledge, Democracy and Higher Education* – zooms in on the civic role of the University, particularly with regard to research and the production of knowledge. In chapter 5 – *Lifelong Learning in the Knowledge Economy* – I analyse recent developments in the field of adult education and lifelong learning in order to show how lifelong learning has become repositioned due to economic demands and considerations. I argue that there is a real danger that, as a result of this, an older connection with democracy will be lost. In chapter 6 – *Towards the Learning Democracy* – I pursue this in more positive terms through the discussion of the work of a number of authors who have explored the relationships between democracy, citizenship, adult education and the public sphere. It is in the context of this discussion that I introduce the idea of the 'learning democracy.' In chapter 7 – *Theorising Civic Learning: Socialisation,*

PROLOGUE

Subjectification and the Ignorant Citizen – I bring the main theoretical threads of the discussion together in order to explore the question what a viable conception of civic learning might look like. I introduce the distinction between a socialisation conception of civic learning and a subjectification conception and make a case that citizenship education needs to be informed by a conception of civic learning and democratic subjectivity that moves beyond a socialisation agenda towards and approach that can truly foster democratic agency.

1

From Teaching Citizenship to Learning Democracy

Over the past decades there has been a world-wide resurgence of interest in questions about education and democratic citizenship, both from the side of educators and educationalists and from the side of policy makers and politicians (for an overview see, for example, Osler & Starkey, 2006). In new and emerging democracies the focus has been on how education can contribute to the formation of democratic citizens and the promotion of a democratic culture, while in established democracies the focus has been on how to nurture and maintain interest in and engagement with democratic processes and practices. At stake in these discussions are not only technical questions about the proper shape and form of education for democratic citizenship but also more philosophical questions about the nature of democracy and the possible configurations of citizenship within democratic societies.

In discussions about the state of democracy two trends can be discerned (see McLaughlin, 2000). On the one hand there are worries about the level of political participation and political understanding, while on the other there are wider concerns about social cohesion and integration. In England the final report by the Advisory Group on Education for Citizenship and the Teaching of Democracy in Schools – known as the Crick Report after its chairman Bernard Crick – not only claimed that there were "worrying levels of apathy, ignorance and cynicism about public life" (Crick, 1998, p. 8) and that the current situation was "inexcusably and damagingly bad" (ibid., p. 16). The report also argued that this situation "could and should be remedied" (ibid., p. 16).

Within these discussions there are particular anxieties about the role and position of young people. The notion that young people have lower levels of political interest, knowledge and behaviour than adults has been well documented. While some argue that this is a normal phenomenon of the life cycle and that political interest increases with age, there is evidence which suggests a decline in political interest and engagement among young people compared to previous generations – at least, that is, with respect to official politics. In response to this some have argued that young people have a different and very distinct political agenda so that a decline in engagement with official politics does not necessarily imply disengagement with social and political issues more generally. Others maintain, however, that young people do not have a distinctive new political agenda of their own.

Although the evidence about levels of political interest and participation is inconclusive, young people, seen as "citizens in the making" (Marshall, 1950, p. 25), have become a principal target of government initiatives aimed at countering the perceived trend of political and social alienation. Citizenship education has become the cornerstone of these initiatives. In England citizenship education was incorporated into the National Curriculum in 1988 as one of the five cross-curricular themes and became a compulsory National Curriculum subject at secondary level for students at Key Stages 3 and 4 (aged 11–16) in 2002. This was complemented by non-statutory guidelines for citizenship education alongside Personal, Social and Health Education (PSHE) at Key Stages 1 and 2 (aged 5–11). In Scotland "responsible citizenship" was listed as one of the four capacities all education should aim to promote and develop in the context of the new national Curriculum for Excellence, launched in 2004 and implemented from 2010 onwards.

While I do not wish to downplay the significance of citizenship education – not in the least because young people themselves have indicated a lack of knowledge and understanding in this area (see, for example, White, Bruce & Ritchie, 2000) – the inclusion of citizenship in the formal curriculum runs the risk of masking a deeper problem concerning young people's citizenship. The point I wish to make in this chapter is that the teaching of citizenship represents at most a partial response to an alleged 'crisis' in democracy. This is why I argue that there is a need to shift the focus of research, policy and practice from the teaching of citizenship towards the different ways in which young people 'learn democracy' through their participation in the contexts and practices that make up their everyday lives, in school, college and university, and in society at large.

The shift from teaching citizenship to learning democracy makes it possible to overcome the individualistic conception of citizenship that underpins much recent thinking in the area of citizenship education. The focus on learning democracy makes it possible to reveal the ways in which such learning is situated in the unfolding lives of young people and how these lives, in turn, are implicated in wider cultural, social, political and economic orders. It ultimately is this wider context which provides opportunities for young people to be democratic citizens – that is to enact their citizenship – and to learn from this. The shift from teaching citizenship to learning democracy emphasises, in other words, that democratic citizenship should not be understood as an attribute of the individual, but invariably has to do with individuals-in-context and individuals-in-relationship. From a research point of view this means that it is only by following young people as they participate in different formal and non-formal practices and settings, and by listening to their voices, that their learning can be adequately understood. This, in turn, makes it possible to acknowledge that the educational responsibility for citizenship learning is not and cannot be confined to schools and teachers but extends to society at large.

I begin this chapter with a reconstruction of the discussion about citizenship and its development in Britain since the Second World War. This reconstruction reveals a shift away from a more comprehensive conception of citizenship that was prominent after the Second World War towards a much more individualistic approach from the 1980s onwards. As a result of this shift, it has become increasingly difficult to acknowledge the situatedness of citizenship. I argue that this trend is also evident in recent developments in citizenship education, most notably in the premise that the alleged crisis in democracy can be adequately addressed by (re)educating individuals.

I outline the problems associated with such an individualistic approach where the emphasis is on the individual per se rather than on the individual-in-context and in-relationship. Against this background I argue for an approach to citizenship education that takes its point of departure in the learning that takes place in the real lives of young people – in school and in society at large. In the concluding section I sketch the implications of this view for research and policy and for the practice of citizenship education.

CITIZENSHIP IN BRITAIN AFTER THE SECOND WORLD WAR

Writing in the aftermath of the Second World War, T.H. Marshall in his essay "Citizenship and Social Class" (Marshall, 1950) delineated a view of citizenship which was to inform the social liberal consensus of the post-war period up to the 1970s. According to Roche (1992, pp. 16–17), Marshall's theoretical framework represents the "dominant paradigm" in citizenship theory in Britain and has continued to represent the touchstone for discussions about citizenship. Mann (1987, p. 34) has even suggested that in relation to Britain Marshall's view of citizenship is "essentially true."

Marshall defined citizenship as "a status bestowed on all those who are full members of a community," and argued that "(a)ll those who possess the status are equal with respect to the rights and duties with which the status is endowed" (Marshall, 1950, pp. 28–29). Marshall took an historical approach which focused on the development of citizenship rights in modern societies. His main thesis was that modern citizenship includes three different kinds of rights: civil, political and social rights. Civil rights, that is the rights necessary for individual freedom, such as "liberty of the person, freedom of speech, thought and faith, the right to own property and to conclude valid contracts, and the right to justice" (ibid., p. 74), developed largely in the eighteenth century. Political rights, including the right to vote and to stand for political office, followed in the nineteenth and early twentieth century. Social rights, which mainly developed in the twentieth century, include "the whole range from the right to a modicum of economic welfare and security to the right to share to the full in the social heritage and to live the life of a civilised being according to the standards prevailing in the society" (ibid., p. 74). According to Marshall each of these kinds of rights corresponds to a particular set of institutions. Civil rights are protected by the court system; political rights correspond to institutions of local government and parliament; while social rights are associated with the welfare state.

Although Marshall's analysis can be read as a description of the development of citizenship rights in Britain, his main concern was with solving the problem of how citizenship and capitalism could be reconciled. The growth in wealth created by capitalism had created the conditions for increasing social rights. Yet, at the very same time these rights posed a threat to the capitalist system since they were collectivist by nature and required increased public expenditure and taxation. For this reason Marshall argued that "in the twentieth century citizenship and the capitalist class system [were] at war" (Marshall, 1950, p. 87). Marshall believed, however, that social rights, institutionalised within the framework of the welfare state, could ultimately mitigate the worst excesses of the market. In line with the functional analysis he was advocating, he introduced the notion of the 'hyphenated society', the constellation of democratic-welfare-capitalism where "the parts are meaningless except in their relationship with one another" (Marshall, 1981, p. 128). Social rights thus rendered citizenship compatible with capitalism by 'civilising' the impact of the market. Fundamentally, he believed that the expansion of social rights would irrevocably ameliorate and cut across class differences and inequalities. Although there was conflict and controversy in the post-war period over the type of policies that were needed to achieve the expansion of citizenship, Marshall's ideas secured "a continued commitment to social justice and social integration through the growth of social rights" (France, 1998, p. 98). Marshall held that with the post-war construction of the welfare state, the progress of citizenship as a rounded and meaningful status was complete.

Notwithstanding the importance of Marshall's work for the understanding and advancement of citizenship in post-war Britain, his ideas have over the past decades been criticised for a number of reasons (for a detailed overview see Faulks, 1998, pp. 42–52). One of the issues Marshall did not explore, was the possibility that the state may work in the interest of one class or group of elites, rather than function as a neutral referee – an assumption which was "naïve even in the context of 1950s Britain" (ibid., p. 44). Faulks concludes, therefore, that although Marshall argued that citizenship requires a social dimension to make it meaningful for most individuals, ultimately the social rights he advocated are "paternalistic and dependent upon the condition of the market economy" (ibid., p. 51). Marshall did not see, in other words, "that meaningful citizenship demands active participation by citizens who possess the necessary resources to facilitate participation" (ibid., p. 51). By failing to transcend the agency-based approach to citizenship, Marshall did not consider "the structural constraints which the market and coercive state place upon the distribution of the resources necessary for citizenship" (ibid., p. 51).

FROM THE WELFARE STATE TO NEO-LIBERALISM

It was, however, not the theoretical weakness of Marshall's arguments that led to a decline in the impact of his thinking. Much more importantly, his optimistic belief in the welfare state as the impartial guarantor of social justice was overtaken by actual transformations in the industrialised world, such as the decline in autonomy of the nation state and the globalisation of production and consumption, and by related social and cultural changes. These developments have radically altered the way in which citizenship is comprehended by individuals and groups in both privileged and marginalised positions.

In Britain, the challenge to the post-war consensus primarily came from the 'New Right' from the mid-1970s onwards. It followed a sustained period of economic and political unrest and was championed by Margaret Thatcher who insisted that a culture of 'welfare dependency' had become endemic in society. Here Thatcher was intuitively following neo-liberal thinkers such as Frederick Hayek, in arguing that social rights and welfare state provision more generally undermine rather than support individual freedom because they weaken personal responsibility and civic virtue. For neo-liberalism "the only way to engender good citizenship is to see as its basis the individual freely choosing to act in a responsible way" (Faulks, 1998, p. 68). This helps to explain why Thatcher sought to counter and reverse the development of social citizenship by returning to the traditional liberal idea of free markets and limited government. She did so, however, within a neo-liberal rather than a classical liberal framework. The difference between the two ideologies is very well captured by Olssen.

> Whereas classical liberalism represents a negative conception of state power in that the individual was to be taken as an object to be freed from the interventions of the state, neoliberalism has come to represent a positive conception of the state's role in creating the appropriate market by providing the conditions, laws and institutions necessary for its operation. In classical liberalism, the individual is characterized as having an autonomous human nature and can practice freedom. In neoliberalism the state seeks to create an individual who is an enterprising and competitive entrepreneur. (Olssen, 1996, p. 340)

The idea of 'limited government' does not mean weak government. The state has to be strong to police and safeguard the market order. Gilmour summarises the apparently contradictory logic of Thatcherite 'authoritarian liberalism' as follows.

> There was no paradox in rhetoric about 'liberty' and the rolling back of the state being combined in practice with centralisation and the expansion of the state's frontiers. The establishment of individualism and a free-market state is an unbending if not dictatorial venture which demands the prevention of collective action and the submission of dissenting institutions and individuals. (Gilmour, 1992, p. 223)

Although the explicit individualistic rhetoric with its "valorization of the individual entrepreneur" (Hall et al., 2000, p. 464) was softened under John Major in the early 1990s, the emphasis on personal responsibility and individual choice was retained. In important areas such as civil service and government reform, the Thatcherite agenda was in fact speeded up under Major.

FROM SOCIAL RIGHTS TO MARKET RIGHTS: THE ACTIVE CITIZEN

The foregoing makes clear that one of the most central aspects of the Conservative governments of Thatcher and Major was the redefinition of the relationship between individuals and the state and hence the redefinition of the very idea of citizenship. Faulks (1998, p. 124) describes the redefinition of citizenship as a shift from social rights to 'market rights,' which comprise "the freedom to choose, the freedom to own property and have property protected, the freedom to spend money as one sees fit, and the right to be unequal." At the centre of this vision stands the active citizen, a 'dynamic individual' who is self-reliant and takes responsibility for his or her own actions, rather than depending upon government intervention and support, and yet possesses 'a sense of civic virtue and pride in both country and local community' (ibid., p. 128). This particular form of active citizenship comprised "a mixture of self-help and voluntarism whereby competition and rigour of market relations would supposedly be 'civilised' by concern for one's community and country" (ibid., p. 128). Although it was underpinned by a perceived need for shared values and reciprocal obligations and loyalties, active citizenship was in effect more concerned with the individual as an autonomous chooser and individual economic consumer in the market place, than with the promotion of community values. Thatcherism, with its individualistic emphasis, only succeeded in increasing social division, rather than creating the basis for community spirit to emerge.

By focusing on the need for individuals to take responsibility for their own actions, the call for active citizenship was based on a particular diagnosis of society's ills, in that it was assumed that what was lacking in society were active and committed individuals. The explanation for society's problems was thus couched in individualistic, psychological and moralistic terms – the result of a lack of individual responsibility, rather than an outcome of more structural causes such as under-funding of welfare state provisions or the loss of political control resulting from privatisation of public services. In this way active citizenship followed the strategy of blaming individuals rather than paying attention to and focusing on the structures that provide the context in which individuals act. Ironically, therefore, active citizenship exemplified a de-politicisation and privatisation of the very idea of citizenship.

CITIZENSHIP AND CAPITALISM

Many analysts see the emergence of the New Right as a radical break with the past, particularly with the social liberal consensus that existed in the first decades after the Second World War. They mainly hold Thatcher responsible for the breakdown of the welfare state and the erosion of social rights. While it is clear that Thatcher had a huge impact on British society – even though she claimed that 'such a thing' did not exist – and while it is also clear that successive Conservative governments had been highly effective in reshaping the political agenda, the demise of the welfare state cannot be exclusively accounted for by a change in political ideology and rhetoric forged by Conservative governments. Faulks suggests that the development of the post-war consensus that gave rise to increased and improved welfare provision and expanded social rights should not simply be understood as a victory of the working class over the ruling class. The development of social rights was also the product of the needs of the ruling class to maintain modern production. The expansion of social citizenship was, in other words, due "to the mutual benefits it secured for capital and labour" (Faulks, 1998, p. 108).

From this point of view, it is hardly surprising that social rights came under pressure when the needs of capitalism changed in the 1970s as a result of the increasing globalisation of production. The relatively brief period of managed capitalism in which production and consumption were mainly confined to the borders of the nation state gave way to a much more anarchic form of global capitalism in which governments were under pressure to offer suitable conditions to global capital in order to remain a player in the global economy. Unlike Marshall's expectations, this created a situation in which the 'war' between citizenship and capitalism returned. Social citizenship, as it had developed in the post-war era, was increasingly seen as an impediment to Britain's competitiveness in the world economy. Viewed from this perspective the Thatcherite agenda of the 1980s can be understood as "an attempt to adjust to the new realities of capitalism by reducing impediments to capitalist investment, such as trade union and social rights, and opening up Britain's economy to increasing globalisation" (Faulks, 1998, p. 121). The neo-liberal ideology of individualism, choice and market rights suited this situation much better than the old ideology of collectivism, solidarity and social rights.

When Labour came to power in May 1997 there were high hopes for a radical change, including the expectation that the welfare state would be rebuilt. These expectations, which were fuelled by the Labour Party itself, have, however, not fully materialised. With respect to citizenship, Labour mainly sought to ameliorate the New Right position by using communitarian ideas to emphasise the importance of social values and social responsibilities. But in key areas such as education and health care – the main pillars of the welfare state – Labour has simply continued with the rhetoric and practice of choice, delivery and accountability, thereby positioning citizens as consumers of 'high quality' social services, rather than as those who participate in democratic decision making about the fair distribution of collective resources (see Biesta, 2004[a]; 2010[a]). In this respect the Labour government continued the individualistic neo-liberal line of thinking that was a prominent feature of preceding Conservative governments.

THE IDEA OF CITIZENSHIP EDUCATION

The foregoing discussion of the development of citizenship in post-war Britain not only provides the factual background for my discussion of the idea of citizenship education. It also serves as a framework for understanding and evaluating recent developments in this field. What it allows me to show is that developments in citizenship education have stayed quite close to the individualistic conception of citizenship that emerged in Britain in the 1980s. Since this is only one of the ways in which the 'problem of citizenship' can be understood, it becomes possible to argue – as I will do below – that the idea of citizenship education as a process of making young people 'ready' for democracy, is only one of the ways in which democratic learning can be promoted and organised, and not necessarily the best way.

Although citizenship education is not a recent invention (see, for example, Batho, 1990), there can be no doubt that in the English context a major impetus for recent initiatives has come from Advisory Group on Education for Citizenship and the Teaching of Democracy in Schools. The brief of this group, set up by the then Secretary of State for Education and Employment, David Blunkett, was "(t)o provide advice on effective education for citizenship in schools – to include the nature and practices of participation in democracy; the duties, responsibilities and rights on individuals as citizens, and the value to individuals and society of community activity" (Crick, 1998, p. 4). The group was also expected to produce "a statement of the aims and purposes of citizenship education in schools" and "a broad framework for what good citizenship in schools might look like, and how it can be successfully delivered' (ibid., p. 4).

The Advisory Group, which consisted of representatives from a very broad political spectrum, argued that effective education for citizenship should consist of three strands. Firstly, social and moral responsibility: "children learning from the very beginning self-confidence and socially and morally responsible behaviour both in and beyond the classroom, both towards those in authority and towards each other" (Crick, 1998, p. 11; emphasis in original). Secondly, community involvement: "learning about and becoming helpfully involved in the life and concerns of their communities, including learning through community involvement and service to the community" (ibid., p. 12; emphasis in original). Thirdly, political literacy: "pupils learning about and how to make themselves effective in public life through knowledge, skills and values" (ibid., p. 13; emphasis in original). Along all three lines the Advisory Group emphasised that citizenship education "is not just knowledge of citizenship and civic society; it also implies developing values, skills and understanding" (ibid., p. 13).

According to Kerr (1999, p. 79), the Advisory Group placed "considerable stress on the outcomes of effective citizenship education ... namely active and responsible participation." What eventually ended up in the Citizenship Order (the official guidelines for the teaching of citizenship), was considerably different to the recommendations of the Advisory Group. This particularly weakened "the holistic impact of the Citizenship Advisory Group's final report" (ibid., p. 79). In the Citizenship Order the following three attainment targets for Key Stages 3 and 4 were specified: (1) Knowledge and understanding about becoming informed citizens; (2) Developing skills of inquiry and approach; (3) Developing skills of participation and responsible action (see ibid., p. 83).

THREE PROBLEMS WITH THE IDEA OF CITIZENSHIP EDUCATION

The framework for citizenship education in England has been criticised from a wide range of different angles (see, for example, Beck, 1998; Garratt, 2000; for a 'temperate' reply see Crick, 2000; see also Crick, 2007). My concern here is not with the specific content and shape of the proposals and practices but with the more general idea of citizenship education, that is, with the idea that an alleged crisis in democracy can be adequately addressed by (re)educating individuals, by making them 'ready' for democratic citizenship through education. I basically see three problems with this line of thinking.

The first problem with the idea of citizenship education is that it is largely aimed at individual young people. The assumption is that they, as individuals, lack the proper knowledge and skills, the right values, and the correct dispositions to be the citizens that they should be. This not only individualises the problem of young people's citizenship – and in doing so follows the neo-liberal line of thinking in which individuals are blamed for their social malfunctioning. It also individualises citizenship itself, most notably through the suggestion that good citizenship will follow from individuals' acquisition of a proper set of knowledge, skills, values and dispositions. One could, of course, argue that citizenship education can only ever be a necessary, but never a sufficient condition for the realisation of good citizenship. This is, for example, acknowledged in the Crick Report, where it is emphasised that "(s)chools can only do so much" and that we "must not ask too little of teachers, but equally we must not ask too much" (Crick, 1998, p. 9). Yet the underlying idea is that schools "could do more" and, more importantly, that they "must be helped" (ibid., p. 9). The latter point suggests that even when the wider context is taken into consideration, it is first and foremost in order to support the effective 'production' of the good citizen.

The second problem I wish to highlight, concerns the assumption that citizenship can be understood as the outcome of an educational trajectory. The idea of citizenship-as-outcome reveals a strong instrumental orientation in the idea of citizenship education. The focus is mainly on the effective means to bring about 'good citizenship' rather on the question what 'good citizenship' actually is or might be. The instrumental orientation clearly comes to the fore in Crick's contention that "(t)he aim of the new subject is to create active and responsible citizens" (Crick, 2000, p. 67; emphasis added). Indeed, the overriding concern has been about how to best engender a particular species of citizenship amongst young people. It has been to find the 'best' and most 'appropriate' methods and approaches of teaching citizenship to young people – of achieving what is regarded to be a common goal that they can aspire to. I therefore agree with Hall et al. (2000, p. 464), that the "contemporary political and policy discussion is for the most part much less concerned to critically interrogate the concept of active citizenship, than it is to debate how such a thing might be achieved." I wish to suggest that a continuous interrogation of the possible meanings of citizenship, a continuous "public dialogue about rival value positions" (Martin & Vincent, 1999, p. 236) should not only be at the very centre of democratic life, but also at the very centre of citizenship education.

The idea of citizenship as outcome is also problematic because it is fabricated on the assumption that citizenship is a status that is only achieved after one has success-fully traversed a specified trajectory. I suggest that citizenship is not so much a status, something which can be achieved and maintained, but that it should primarily be understood as something that people continuously do: citizenship as practice (see Lawy & Biesta, 2006). Citizenship is, in other words, not an identity that someone can 'have,' but first and foremost a practice of identification, more specifically a practice of identification with public issues, that is, with issues that are of a common concern. This implies that a culture of participation should be a central and essential element of democratic citizenship.

As long as citizenship is conceived as outcome, it places young people in the problematic position of not-yet-being-a-citizen. Indeed, as France has argued, citizenship "is generally understood as an adult experience" and, as a result, being young is only seen as "a transitional stage between 'childhood' and 'adulthood'" (France, 1998, p. 99). Such an approach, set alongside my concerns about citizenship as outcome, fails to recognise that young people always already participate in social life; that their lives are implicated in the wider social, economic, cultural and political world; and they are not isolated from these processes. In effect, being a citizen involves much more than the simple acquisition of certain fixed core values and dispositions. It is participative and as such it is itself an inherently educative process as it has to do with the transformation of the ways in which young people relate to, understand and express their place and role in society.

This is precisely the point where the question of learning arises – which brings me to the third and final problem with the idea of citizenship education. One obvious problem with any educational strategy, including the teaching of citizenship, is that there is no guarantee that what young people learn is identical to what is being taught. Proponents of the idea of 'effective' education may want us to believe that it is only a matter of time before research provides us with evidence about the teaching strategies that will guarantee 'success.' Yet apart from the question what counts as 'success' and who has the right to define it, they seem to forget that what students learn from what they are being taught crucially depends on the ways they interpret and make sense of the teaching, something they do on the basis of a wide and diverge range of experiences (see Biesta, 1994; Bloomer, 1997). Education is a process of communication, which relies upon the active acts of meaning making of students and it is this unpredictable factor which makes education possible in the first place (see Vanderstraeten & Biesta, 2001; Biesta, 2004[b]). Moreover, young people learn at least as much about democracy and citizenship from their participation in the range of different practices that make up their lives, as they learn from that which is officially prescribed and formally taught. Even where a school includes exceptional internal democratic arrangements – such as a school council or other ways in which young people are enabled to participate meaningfully in the collective decision making about their educational experience – this still only represents a small proportion of the environment in and from which young people learn. They learn as much, and most possibly even more, from their participation in the family or leisure activities, from interaction with their peers, from the media, from advertising and from their role as consumers – and they often learn different and even contradictory things (see also Biesta, Lawy & Kelly, 2009).

All this suggests that the learning of democratic citizenship is situated within the lives of young people. The way in which young people make sense of their experiences – including their experience of citizenship education – depends crucially upon their own perspectives which are, in turn, shaped by the outcomes of previous learning and meaning-making (see Dewey, 1938[a]). But young people's perspectives – and hence their learning and action in the area of democratic citizenship – are also influenced by the wider cultural, social, political and economic order that impacts upon their lives. It is at this point that the individualistic approach to citizenship education and the individualistic understanding of citizenship itself reveals one of its main shortcomings as it tends to forget – or at least downplays the significance of – the situations in which young people live and act. As France (1998) has argued, it is not enough to expect or to enforce young people to become active citizens.

As a society we have to recognise that young people need a stake in the society or community in which they live. During the last 15 years this has been reduced by the erosion of social rights and the expression of social power by certain adults. This has led to fewer opportunities in both the community and employ-ment for young people to move into the adult world. It is important therefore to recognise that without these opportunities many young people will not feel any desire to undertake social responsibility either to their local or national community. (France, 1998, pp. 109–110)

I agree with France that the 'problem' of citizenship is misunderstood if it is con-ceived as an abstract unwillingness of young people to become active in social and political life. The problem always has to be constructed as one of young-people-in-context, which means that it is as much about the young people as it is about the context in which they live and learn. It is, in other words, the actual condition of young people's citizenship which has a crucial – and perhaps even decisive – impact upon the ways in which young people can be citizens and upon the ways in which they learn democratic citizenship.

CONCLUSIONS: FROM TEACHING CITIZENSHIP TO LEARNING DEMOCRACY

In this chapter I have provided an overview of the evolution of the theory and practice of citizenship in post-war Britain. Against this background I have discussed recent initiatives in citizenship education in England, focusing on the general thrust of the idea of citizenship education. Although I do not wish to argue against citizenship education – schools can make a difference – I have suggested that the prevailing approach to the teaching of citizenship is problematic for two related reasons. On the one hand this has to do with the fact that the 'problem' of citizenship is mainly understood as a problem of individuals and their behaviour. On the other hand it is because the response to the 'problem' of citizenship so conceived focuses mainly on individuals and their knowledge, skills and dispositions. I have argued that the problem of citizenship is not about young people as individuals but about young people-in-context which is why citizenship education should not only focus on young people as isolated individuals but on young people-in-relationship and on the social, economic, cultural and political conditions of their lives. This suggests a different direction not only for citizenship education itself, but also for research and policy. My case for a shift from teaching citizenship to learning democracy is meant as a marker of such a change in direction.

One of the main implications for research lies in the need to focus on the ways in which young people actually learn democracy. It requires research which aims to understand the various ways in which young people can actually be democratic citizens and learn from this. It asks, in other words, for a contextualised understanding of the ways in which young people learn democracy, one which gives a central role to their actual 'condition of citizenship'. It is only by following young people as they move in and out of different contexts, practices and institutions and by trying to understand what they learn from their participation, or non-participation, in these contexts, that we can actually begin to understand what is going in the lives of young citizens in Britain today (for an example of such an approach see Biesta, Lawy & Kelly, 2009).

The shift from teaching citizenship to learning democracy also has implications for policy makers and politicians. If policy makers and politicians are really concerned about young people's democratic citizenship, they should pay attention to and, even more importantly, invest in the actual conditions under which young people can be citizens and can learn what it means to be a citizen. What I have in mind, here, is not only investment in economic terms, although the resources that make real and meaningful participation of all citizens, including young citizens, possible, are of crucial importance for the ways in which young people can learn democracy. Policy makers and politicians also need to invest in a different way, in that they need to think very carefully about the impact of their policies and strategies on young people's perceptions of democracy and citizenship. What, for example, do young people learn from the fact that the government's interest in education only seems to be about test-scores and performance in a small number of academic subjects? What do young people learn from the fact that the government supports an educational system where those with money have a much better chance of success in life? And how does the experience of unemployment, poverty and bad housing impact upon young people living under these conditions? There are powerful 'lessons in citizenship' to be learned in everyday life which means that the educational responsibility cannot and does not stop at the point where an effective system of citizenship teaching is in place. The educational responsibility extends to the very conditions of young people's citizenship, because these conditions define the context in which they will learn what it means to be a democratic citizen.

Finally, the shift from teaching citizenship to learning democracy also has important implications for citizenship education itself. One implication is that questions about the definition of citizenship should not be kept outside of citizenship education, but should be part and parcel of what citizenship education is about. What constitutes 'good citizenship' is not something that can be defined by politicians and educationalists and then simply set as an aim for young people to achieve. This does not mean that citizenship education should only be about the exploration of the possible meanings of citizenship. If learning democracy is situated in the lives of young people, then citizenship education should also facilitate a critical examination of the actual conditions of young people's citizenship, even it leads them to the conclusion that their own citizenship is limited and restricted. Such an approach would provide the basis for a much deeper understanding of and engagement with democratic citizenship than what lessons in citizenship might be able to achieve.

2

Curriculum, Citizenship and Democracy

In the previous chapter I have highlighted that recent thinking about the relationships between education, democracy and citizenship is strongly individualistic in outlook. This is not only reflected in the way in which politicians and policy makers tend to see the *problem* of citizenship as being first and foremost a problem of individuals and their attitudes and behaviours. It is also visible in educational initiatives that focus on the transformation of children and young people into good and contributing citizens. I have indicated several shortcomings of this way of thinking, both with regard to the conception of democratic citizenship that underlies this approach – a conception which I have characterised as 'citizenship-as-status' – and with regard to the views of education that are at stake –which are captured in the idea of 'citizenship-as-outcome.' Against this background I have argued for a shift in research, policy and practice from the teaching of citizenship to the many ways in which children and young people learn democracy through their engagement in the practices and processes that make up their everyday lives. This view is informed by the idea of 'citizenship-as-practice' and emphasises the crucial role of the actual condition of young people's citizenship for their formation as democratic citizens. While the teaching of citizenship may have a role to play in young people's democratic learning, this learning is always mediated by what children and young people experience in their everyday lives about democratic ways of acting and being and about their own position as citizens – experiences that are not always necessarily positive.

In this chapter I wish to continue the analysis of the theory and practice of citizenship education by looking in more detail at recent developments in Scotland. While much attention has been paid to the introduction of citizenship in the English National Curriculum, far less is known about Scotland. The main reason for focusing on the Scottish case is because, unlike in England where citizenship has become a additional curriculum subject, the new Scottish National Curriculum has citizenship as one of the four capacities that are supposed to permeate all educational activity for children and young people of all ages. The approach to citizenship in the Scottish Curriculum for Excellence is therefore less about teaching and more about experiences that are relevant for the formation of democratic citizenship. While this has the potential to bring educational practice closer to the ways in which children and young people learn democracy, much depends on the views on citizenship and democracy that inform the Scottish curriculum. In this chapter I therefore provide a critical analysis of the views of citizenship and democracy that can be found in the Scottish Curriculum for Excellence, not only in order to highlight the choices that have been made but also to show some of the limitations of the more integrated or embedded approach taken in Scotland.

RESPONSIBLE CITIZENSHIP

The Scottish *Curriculum for Excellence* lists 'responsible citizenship' as one of the four capacities which it envisages that all children and young people should develop. "Our aspiration," as it was put in the foreword by the then Minister and Deputy Minister for Education and Young People to the 2004 *Curriculum for Excellence* document, "is to enable all children to develop their capacities as successful learners, confident individuals, responsible citizens and effective contributors to society" (SE, 2004, p. 3). *Curriculum for Excellence* provides the overall framework for this ambition by enlisting the values, outlining the purposes and articulating the principles for curriculum design that should inform all education from the age of 3 to the age of 18. In the document responsible citizens are depicted as individuals who have "respect for others" and a "commitment to participate responsibly in political, economic, social and cultural life" and who are able to "develop knowledge and understanding of the world and Scotland's place in it; understand different beliefs and cultures; make informed choices and decisions; evaluate environmental, scientific and technological issues; [and] develop informed, ethical views of complex issues" (ibid., p. 12).

Scotland has not been unique in its attempt to put citizenship on the educational agenda although compared to other countries it can actually be said to be rather late in doing this (see Andrews & Mycock, 2007). There are, however, aspects of the Scottish trajectory and approach which are distinctive – particularly the fact that Scotland has not chosen to make citizenship education into a separate curriculum subject and the fact that *Curriculum for Excellence* depicts citizenship as a 'capacity' – and these warrant further exploration. This can not only help to better understand the specific character of the approach taken within Scottish education for citizenship but can also shed light on the strengths and weaknesses of this particular approach. The main purpose of this chapter, therefore, is to analyse and characterise the conception of citizenship education articulated in the context of *Curriculum for Excellence* and to locate this conception within the wider literature on education, citizenship, and democracy. This will make it possible to investigate the assumptions informing the Scottish approach and to highlight the choices made. The view on citizenship pursued in the context of *Curriculum for Excellence* is, after all, not neutral or inevitable – it is not something that 'just is' (Ross & Munn, 2008, p. 270) – but rather represents a particular position within the available spectrum of conceptions of democratic citizenship and citizenship education.

EDUCATION FOR CITIZENSHIP IN SCOTLAND

Although there has always been attention for the role of education in the development of citizenship – the Modern Studies curriculum from 1962, for example, encompassed current affairs and the development of political literacy (see Andrews & Mycock, 2007, p. 74) – the field received a new impetus as a result of the establishment of the Scottish Parliament in 1999. Early on the Scottish Executive announced five National Priorities for schools in Scotland. Priority number 4 focused on values and citizenship and "echoed developments in England" but "with a distinctively Scottish interpretation, not least the emphasis on *education for citizenship*, rather than *citizenship education*" (Blee and McClosky, 2003, p. 3; see also Mannion, 2003 on the distinction between education *for* and education *as* citizenship). In 1999 the Scottish Executive and the Scottish Consultative Council on the Curriculum (now: Learning and Teaching Scotland) set up a working group to focus on education for citizenship. The group produced a discussion and consultation paper in 2000 (LTS, 2000) and a more detailed paper "for discussion and development" in 2002 (LTS, 2002). The then Minister for Education and Young People endorsed the latter paper "as the basis for a national framework for education for citizenship from 3 to 18" (LTS, 2002, p. 2) and commended it "for adoption and use in ways appropriate to local needs and circumstances" (ibid.). In 2003 HM Inspectorate for Education published a follow-up document intended to assist schools in evaluating the quality and effectiveness of their provision for education for citizenship (HMIE, 2003). In 2004 the Scottish Executive published *A Curriculum for Excellence* (SE, 2004) which, as mentioned, presented the capacity for responsible citizenship as one of the four purposes of the curriculum from 3–18 (SE, 2004, p. 12). In 2006 HM Inspectorate for Education published a "portrait" of current practice in education for citizenship in Scottish schools and pre-school centres (HMIE, 2006a), followed by a similar report on provision in Scotland's colleges (HMIE, 2006b).

I consider Learning and Teaching Scotland's 2002 paper *Education for Citizenship in Scotland: A paper for discussion and development* the most central publication of this list, not only because it is the most detailed in its account of what citizenship is and how education can contribute to the development of the capacity for citizenship, but also because it became the official framework for further developments in the field, and clearly influenced the positioning of citizenship within *Curriculum for Excellence*. The contributions of HMIE are, however, also important, most notably because of the fact that education for citizenship in Scotland is driven by rather broad outcomes and not by specified input. As a result the Inspectorate is likely to have a much stronger influence on educational practice as it needs to judge the quality of many different operationalisations of the outcomes, than in those cases where its main task consists of checking the implementation of a pre-specified curriculum. This, in turn, highlights the importance of the particular interpretation of HMIE of the framing documents. The *Curriculum for Excellence* document occupies a middle position in all this. It is less detailed on citizenship than the 2002 *Education for Citizenship* paper because it had to cover all purposes and outcomes of education. Its specific interpretation of earlier documents is, nonetheless, significant because of its role as a framework for Scottish education from 3 to 18. What, then, is the particular view on citizenship and education for citizenship in the 2002 *Education for Citizenship* document, and how has this been taken up and further developed in Curriculum for Excellence and HMIE reports and activities?

The foreword to the *Education for Citizenship* document summarises the central idea of the paper as "that young people should be enabled to develop capability for thoughtful and responsible participation in political, economic, social and cultural life" (LTS, 2002, p. 3). This is said to depend on the development of four aspects: "knowledge and understanding, skills and competence, values and dispositions and creativity and enterprise" (ibid.). This, in turn, is related to two 'core themes.' The first is the idea that "young people learn most about citizenship by being active citizens" (ibid.). This requires that schools should model the kind of society in which active citizenship is encouraged "by providing all young people with opportunities to take responsibility and exercise choice" (ibid.). The second is that the development of capability for citizenship "should be fostered in ways that motivate young people to be active and responsible members of their communities – local, national and global" (ibid.).

These sentences reveal in a nutshell what I see as the four defining characteristics of the Scottish approach to education for citizenship. The first is that there is a strong *individualistic tendency* in the approach, exemplified in the fact that citizenship is depicted as a capacity or capability, based upon a particular set of knowledge, skills and dispositions and understood in terms of individual responsibility and choice. The second is that the approach is based on a *broad conception of the domain of citizenship* which encompasses political, economic, social and cultural life. The third is the emphasis on *activity*, both with regard to the exercise of citizenship as active citizenship and with regard to the ways in which citizenship can be learned, viz., through engagement in citizenship activity. The fourth is a strong emphasis on the (idea of) *community* as the relevant environment or setting for the exercise and development of citizenship. I will discuss the first two characteristics in some detail and will then make more brief comments about the other two.

INDIVIDUALISM

The individualistic take on citizenship and citizenship education is clearly exemplified in the 2002 *Education for Citizenship* document. It opens by saying that "(s)chools and other educational establishments have a central part to play in educating young people for life as active and responsible members of their communities" (LTS, 2002, p. 6), thus reiterating the idea that citizenship resides first and foremost in a *personal* responsibility. The document depicts citizenship responsibility as the corollary of citizenship rights. Citizenship involves "enjoying rights and exercising responsibilities" and these "are reciprocal in many respects" (ibid., p. 8). The document emphasises that young people should be regarded "as citizens of today rather than citizens in waiting," an idea which is linked to the *UN Convention on the Rights of the Child* which states that children "are born with rights" (ibid.). The individualistic tendency is also clearly exemplified in the overall goal of citizenship education which "should aim to develop capability for thoughtful and responsible participation in political, economic, social and cultural life," a capability which is considered to be rooted in "*knowledge and understanding*, in a range of *generic skills and competences*, including 'core skills', and in a variety of *personal qualities and dispositions*" (ibid., p. 11; emphasis in original). The document seems to hint at a distinction between necessary and sufficient conditions for citizenship, arguing, for example, that "being a capable citizen" is not just about possessing knowledge and skills but also about "being able and willing to use knowledge and skills to make decisions and, where appropriate, take action" (ibid., p. 11). Similarly, "effective citizenship" is not just about having the capacity and dispositions to be active, but it is also about "being able to take action and make things happen" (ibid.). Capability for citizenship is therefore said to depend on a number of literacies: social, economic and cultural and also political (see ibid.). In doing so it pursues a common way of thinking about the possibilities of education for citizenship, namely one in which it is argued that education can work on (some of) the necessary conditions for citizenship, but, on its own, will never be sufficient for the development of effective and involved citizenship. This is why "the contributions of formal education need to be seen alongside, and in interaction with, other influences" from, for example, "parents, carers and the media and opportunities for community-based learning" (ibid., pp. 9–10).

The 2002 *Education for Citizenship* document analyses the capability for citizenship in terms of four related outcomes which are all seen as aspects or attributes of individuals.

Knowledge and understanding is concerned with "the need to base opinions, views and decisions on relevant knowledge and on a critical evaluation and balanced interpretation of evidence" (ibid., p. 12). Knowledgeable citizens are aware "of the complexities of the economic, ethical and social issues and dilemmas that confront people" and "have some knowledge of political, social, economic and cultural ideas and phenomena" (ibid., p. 12).

Education for citizenship involves developing a range of *skills and competencies* "that need to be developed along with various personal qualities such as self-esteem, confidence, initiative, determination and emotional maturity in order to be responsible and effective participants in a community" (ibid., p. 13). Being skilled and competent means "feeling empowered [and] knowing and valuing one's potential for positive action" (ibid.).

Values and dispositions: Education for citizenship also involves "developing the ability to recognise and respond thoughtfully to values and value judgements that are part and parcel of political, economic, social and cultural life" (ibid., p. 13). Also, education can help to foster "a number of personal qualities and dispositions rooted in values of respect and care for self, for others and for the environment" and promoting "a sense of social responsibility" (ibid., p. 13).

Being an 'effective citizen' is also supposed to entail the capacity for "thinking and acting creatively in political, economic, social and cultural life" and "being enterprising in one's approach to participation in society" (ibid., p. 14).

Finally, the document mentions the need for the development of "the integrative ability that is at the heart of effective and purposeful citizenship" (ibid., p. 14) so as to make sure that the four outcomes are not developed in isolation.

While all this points towards a strong emphasis on individuals and on citizenship as an individual responsibility and capacity – something which is further exemplified by the strong emphasis on the development of values such as "respect and care for people and a sense of social and environmental responsibility" (ibid., p. 11) – there are some other aspects of the 2002 *Education for Citizenship* document which

21

point in a different direction. Most significant in this regard is a passage in which it is acknowledged that "(w)hilst all individuals share the rights and responsibilities of citizenship, regardless of status, knowledge or skill, it is clear that citizenship may be exercised with different degrees of effectiveness" (ibid., p. 9). This variety is attributed both to personal and to social circumstances. Here, the document refers, for example, to homelessness as a factor which may impede (young) people from exercising their citizenship rights, just as "poverty and other forms of disadvantage" may impact on the capacity for effective citizenship. The document therefore concludes that it is in the interest both of individuals and of society as a whole "that rights and responsibilities of citizenship are well understood, that young people develop the capability needed to function effectively as citizens in modern society" and "*that structures are provided to enable them to do so*" (ibid.; my emphasis). Within the 2002 *Education for Citizenship* document this is, however, one of the few places where the possibility of a structural dimension of citizenship – and by implication a responsibility for citizenship that does *not* lie with the individual but rather with the state – is being considered. The general thrust of the document, however, is on the individual and his or her actions and responsibilities.

This line of thinking is continued in the *Curriculum for Excellence* document where 'responsible citizenship' figures as one of the four capacities which the curriculum from 3–18 should enable all children and young people to develop (SE, 2004, p. 12). *Curriculum for Excellence* is explicit and upfront about the values which should inform education. It reminds its readers of the fact that the words "wisdom, justice, compassion and integrity ... are inscribed on the mace of the Scottish Parliament" and that these "have helped to define values for our democracy" (ibid., p. 11). Hence it is seen as "one of the prime purposes of education to make our young people aware of the values on which Scottish society is based and so help them to establish their own stances on matters of social justice and personal and collective responsibility" (ibid.). Therefore, young people "need to learn about and develop these values" (ibid.). To achieve this, the curriculum "should emphasise the rights and responsibilities of individuals and nations"; "should help young people to understand diverse cultures and beliefs and support them in developing concern, tolerance, care and respect for themselves and others"; "must promote a commitment to considered judgement and ethical action" and "should give young people the confidence, attributes and capabilities to make valuable contributions to society" (ibid.). Although the *Curriculum for Excellence* document acknowledges what we might call the situated character of citizenship, its depiction as value-based, its articulation in terms of responsibility, respect and commitment to responsible participation, plus the fact that it is embedded in capacity-based conception of education all highlight the strong individualistic tendency in the conception of citizenship and citizenship education.

One of the most interesting aspects of the 2006 HMIE publication *Education for Citizenship* (HMIE, 2006a) is that it combines ideas from the 2002 *Education for Citizenship* discussion and consultation paper with the *Curriculum for Excellence* framework. The result is a view of citizenship and citizenship education which is (even) more strongly individualistic than was the case in the two documents upon which it is based. This is first of all because the HMIE document argues that the other three capacities of the *Curriculum for Excellence* framework – confident individuals, effective contributors and successful learners – are a precondition, or at least an important part of, the development of the capacity for responsible citizenship (see HMIE, 2006a, p. 1). Secondly, it is because the HMIE document gives a prominent position to the development of citizenship *skills* which, by their very nature, are 'tied' to the individual – an idea which becomes even more central in the HMIE paper on *Citizenship in Scotland's Colleges* (HMIE, 2006b). Thirdly, the HMIE document presents education for citizenship as a form of values education (see HMIE, 2006a, p. 3), and in this context emphasises the importance of the development of personal values which, in the document, encompass political, social, environmental and spiritual values (see ibid.). Finally, the document emphasises that education for citizenship "must enable learners to become critical and independent thinkers" (ibid.), something which it also links to the development of "life skills" (ibid.). The framing of the approach presented in this document is therefore strongly focused on individuals and their attributes, skills and values. This is not to suggest that the document only pays attention to these aspects of citizenship. In the 'portraits' and 'examples of effective practice' there is also discussion of such things as the involvement and participation of children and young people in decision making, both with regard to their learning and in the context of pupils' councils, the importance of the school ethos, engagement with community and voluntary organisations, and attention for global issues. There is also a strong emphasis on environmental issues and on the Eco-Schools scheme as providing important opportunities for citizenship learning.

THE DOMAIN OF CITIZENSHIP

Whereas the conception of citizenship as a capacity based upon responsible action of individuals is clearly individualistic, and whereas the emphasis of the educational efforts on the development of knowledge, skills and dispositions has a strong focus on individuals and their traits and attributes as well, this is mitigated within the Scottish approach by a strong emphasis on the need for experiential learning within the domain of citizenship. All documents agree that the best way to learn citizenship is, as it is put in the 2002 Education for Citizenship document, "through experience and interaction with others" (LTS, 2002, p. 10). "In short, learning about citizenship is best achieved by being an active citizen." (ibid.) This idea is one of the main reasons why the approach proposed in the document "does not involve the creation of a new subject called 'citizenship education'" (ibid., p. 16). Instead, the document takes the view "that each young person's entitlement to education for citizenship can be secured through combinations of learning experiences set in the daily life of the school, discrete areas of the curriculum, cross-curricular experiences and activities involving links with the local community" (ibid.). The ethos of education for citizenship is therefore explicitly "active" and "participatory" and based on opportunities for "active engagement" (ibid.). This view, which is further supported by the idea that young people should be regarded "as citizens of today rather than citizens in waiting" (ibid., p. 8), raises a crucial question, which is about the kind of communities and activities considered to be relevant for citizenship learning. What, in other words, is considered to be the domain for citizenship and, hence, for education for citizenship and citizenship learning.

The first thing to note is that most documents denote this domain in broad terms. In the 2002 *Education for Citizenship* document the overall purpose of education for citizenship is defined as "thoughtful and responsible participation in political, economic, social and cultural life" (LTS, 2002, p. 11; see also p. 3, p. 5). A similar phrase is used in *Curriculum for Excellence* where responsible citizens are individuals with a commitment "to participate responsibly in political, economic, social and cultural life" (SE, 2004, p. 12). This is echoed in the HMIE document (HMIE, 2006a) where the purpose of education for citizenship is described as "to prepare young people for political, social, economic, cultural and educational participation in society" (HMIE, 2006a, p. 2). Whereas several of the documents include questions about the environment in their conception of the domain of citizenship, the HMIE document is the only document discussed in this chapter which makes mention of spiritual values alongside political, social and environmental values as the set of values that education for citizenship should seek to promote (see ibid., p. 3), albeit that a reference to religion is remarkable absent in the discussion.

The broad conception of the citizenship domain represents a clear choice on behalf of the authors of the 2002 *Education for Citizenship* document. The document starts from the assumption that everyone belongs to various types of community, "both communities of place, from local to global, and communities of interest, rooted in common concern or purpose" (LTS, 2002, p. 8). Against this background citizenship is said to involve "enjoying rights and responsibilities in these various types of community" (ibid.). The document then adds that this way of seeing citizenship "encompasses the specific idea of political participation by members of a democratic state" but it also includes "the more general notion that citizenship embraces a range of participatory activities, not all overtly political, that affect the welfare of communities" (ibid.). Examples of the latter type of citizenship include "voluntary work, personal engagement in local concerns such as neighbourhood watch schemes or parent-teacher associations, or general engagement in civic society" (ibid.).

What is important to acknowledge about this articulation of the domain of citizenship is that citizenship *encompasses* participation in political processes but is not confined to it. Thus, the Scottish approach is based on what we might call a *social* rather than an exclusively political conception of citizenship, one which understands citizenship in terms of membership of and concern for the many communities that make up people's lives. This includes the more narrowly political domain of citizenship, but extends to civil society and potentially includes any community. This is why "active and responsible citizenship" is said to have to do with "individuals having a sense of belonging to, and functioning in, communities" (ibid., p. 9). The question this raises is what the role of the political dimension in the Scottish conception of citizenship actual is. This not only has to do with the extent to which citizenship is related to questions about the (democratic) quality of collective decision making, but also concerns questions about the relationships between citizens, the relationships between citizens and the state, and the role of the state more generally in relation to its citizens. It is at this point that the documents begin to diverge.

The 2002 *Education for Citizenship* document is the most explicit about the political dimensions of and rationale for education for citizenship. It explicitly links the need for education for citizenship to the "advent of the Scottish Parliament" which has encouraged a 'fresh focus' on the importance of people living in Scotland "being able to understand and participate in democratic processes" (ibid., p. 6). Here citizenship is connected to the functioning of a democratic society and education for citizenship is brought in connection with concerns about "disaffection and disengagement from society" (ibid.). It is therefore concluded that education "has a key role to play in fostering a modern democratic society, whose members have a clear sense of identity and belonging, feel empowered to participate effectively in their communities and recognise their roles and responsibilities as global citizens" (ibid., p. 7). The need for education for citizenship is also linked to the development of "a healthy and vibrant culture of democratic participation" (ibid., p. 9) and within this context the document emphasises the need for understanding "that perceptions of rights and responsibilities by individuals in different social groups are sometimes in conflict" (ibid., p. 8), so that education for citizenship must help young people "develop strategies for dealing effectively with controversy" (ibid., p. 9). This is explicitly linked to democratic skills and dispositions such as "negotiation, compromise, awareness of the impact of conflict on the overall wellbeing of the community and the environment, and development of well-informed respect for differences between people" (ibid., p. 9).

Awareness of the political dimensions of citizenship is also clear in the description of the 'knowledge and understanding' dimension of education for citizenship as this includes knowledge and understanding of "the rights and responsibilities underpinning democratic societies; opportunities for individuals and voluntary groups to bring about social and environmental change, and the values on which such endeavours are based; (...) the causes of conflict and possible approaches to resolving it, recognising that controversy is normal in society and sometimes has beneficial effects" (ibid., p. 12). The 'values and dispositions' outcome makes mention of a disposition to "develop informed and reasoned opinions about political, economic, social and environmental issues" and a disposition to "understand and value social justice, recognising that what counts as social justice is itself contentious" (ibid., p. 14). When the document begins to address "effective education for citizenship in practice" (ibid., pp. 16–31) the emphasis on the more political dimensions of citizenship begins to be replaced by a conception of citizenship as having to do with inclusive and participatory ways of social interaction in a range of communities, but not necessarily or explicitly in the context of political and democratic practices and processes. Here, citizenship begins to veer towards active involvement in environmental projects and community service – a form of 'good deeds' citizenship – where the political dimension and purpose seems to have become largely absent. The 2002 *Education for Citizenship* document moves from a more political to a more social conception of citizenship, and although it is clear about its choice for a more encompassing conception of citizenship which includes the political but extends to the social, it is far less clear about its rationale for *why* community involvement, doing good deeds and, in a sense, being an obedient and contributing citizen, constitutes citizenship – or to be more precise: constitutes good and desirable citizenship.

Although the Curriculum for Excellence document is shorter and far more general than the Education for Citizenship paper, and although, as I have shown above, it does locate questions about citizenship within a wider, political context, its articulation of the abilities involved in responsible citizenship lacks an explicit political and democratic dimension and is predominantly at the social end of the spectrum. Responsible citizens are depicted as individuals who have "respect for others" and a "commitment to participate responsibly in political, economic, social and cultural life" and who are able to "develop knowledge and understanding of the world and Scotland's place in it; understand different beliefs and cultures; make informed choices and decisions; evaluate environmental, scientific and technological issues; [and] develop informed, ethical views of complex issues" (SE, 2004, p. 12).

The social orientation is even more prominent in the HMIE Education for Citizenship document (HMIE, 2006a). Although some reference to democratic processes, the Scottish Youth Parliament and issues "such as social justice and human rights" is made, citizenship is depicted predominantly in relation to society at large, with a strong emphasis on the involvement of pupils in decision making at school level and, to a lesser extent, the wider community. This reveals that from the perspective of HMIE the school is seen as the most relevant and prominent citizenship domain and the most important citizenship 'modus' is that of active involvement and participation. What is mostly lacking is a connection of citizenship with the political domain, both in terms of the 'scope' of citizenship and in terms of the way in which relevant learning processes are understood and depicted. The HMIE document thus represents a strong emphasis on the social dimensions of citizenship and is therefore even more strongly located at the social end of the citizenship spectrum.

ACTIVE CITIZENSHIP

Although the social dimension of citizenship and an emphasis on participation and active involvement are not unimportant for the development of citizenship knowledge and dispositions, and although an emphasis on the social dimensions of citizenship is definitely important for the preservation and maintenance of civil society, an almost exclusive emphasis on these aspects runs the danger that the political dimensions of citizenship, including an awareness of the limitations of personal responsibility for effective political action and change, remain invisible and become unattainable for children and young people. There is the danger, in other words, that citizenship becomes de-politicised and that, as a result, students are not sufficiently empowered to take effective political action in a way that goes beyond their immediate concerns and responsibilities. There is a similar danger with regard to the third aspect of the Scottish approach: the strong emphasis on activity and active citizenship. On the one hand, the idea of active citizenship is important and significant, both with regard to understanding what citizenship is and entails and with regard to citizenship learning. As I have argued in the previous chapter, the most significant citizenship learning that takes place in the lives of young people is the learning that follows from their actual experiences and their actual 'condition' of citizenship. These experiences, which are part of the lives they lead inside and outside of the school, can be said to form the real citizenship curriculum for young people, which shows the crucial importance of opportunities for positive experiences with democratic action and decision making in all aspects of young people's lives. In this regard I do very much agree with the claim made in the 2002 *Education for Citizenship* document that "young people learn most about citizenship by being active citizens" (LTS, 2002, p. 3). But the crucial question here is what young people's active citizenship actually entails.

As I have already argued in the previous section, this depends partly on the domain in which citizenship activity is exercised. But it also depends on the nature of the activity. In this regard it is important not to lose sight of the specific history of the idea of active citizenship which, as discussed in the previous chapter, was introduced by conservative governments in the late 1980s and early 1990s as a way to let citizens take care of what used to be the responsibility of the government under welfare state conditions. While it is difficult to argue against active citizenship, it is important, therefore, to be precise about the nature of the activity and the domain in which the activity is exercised. Active citizenship in itself can either operate at the social or at the political end of the citizenship spectrum and can therefore either contribute to politicisation and the development of political literacy, or be basically a- or non-political. Given the different views on the domain of citizenship it is, therefore, not entirely clear how political and enabling active citizenship within the Scottish context will be, although the tendency seems to be on a form of active citizenship located towards the social end of the citizenship spectrum.

COMMUNITY

The fourth and final characteristic of the Scottish approach to citizenship and education for citizenship is a strong emphasis on community – and it is perhaps significant that in the 2002 *Education for Citizenship* document the word 'community' is used 76 times and the word 'communities' 31 times, while the word 'democratic' is used 9 times and the word 'democracy' only once. The 2002 *Education for Citizenship* document, as I have already mentioned, opens by saying that "(s)chools and other educational establishments have a central part to play in educating young people for life as active and responsible members of their communities" (LTS, 2002, p. 6). The point I wish to raise here is not about the fact that citizenship is depicted in relation to (local, and sometimes also global) communities, but concerns the particular way in which communities are conceived within the documents. In all documents 'community' is used as an unproblematic notion and generally also as a positive notion. The documents speak about young people and *their* communities, suggesting not only that it is clear what these communities are, but also suggesting that young people's membership of these communities is obvious and taken for granted. An important question, however, is what actually constitutes a community and what the difference might be between a social, a cultural and a political community.

As I have argued elsewhere in more detail (see Biesta, 2004[c]; 2006) there is a strong tendency within the literature on communities to think of communities in

27

terms of sameness, commonality and identity. This may be true for many cultural and, perhaps to a lesser extent, social communities – and it seems to be the conception of community implied in most of what the documents have to say about community. But whereas cultural and social communities may display a strong sense of commonality and sameness, this is not how we should understand *political* communities. One could argue – and many political philosophers have argued this point – that the very purpose of politics, and more specifically democratic politics, is to deal in one way or another with the fact of plurality, with the fact that individuals within society have different conceptions of the good life, different values, and different ideas about what matters to them. Ultimately, political communities are therefore communities that are characterised by plurality and difference (see Biesta, 2004[c]), and it is precisely here that the difficulty of politics and 'political existence' (Biesta, 2010[b]) is located. Whereas, as I have shown in my discussion of the domain of citizenship, there is some awareness within the documents, particularly the earlier parts of the 2002 *Education for Citizenship* document, of the particular nature of political communities and political existence – most notably in the recognition of the plurality of perceptions of rights and responsibilities (see LTS, 2002, pp. 8–9) – the predominant conception of community in the documents is that of the community as a community of sameness (for a similar conclusion see Ross & Munn, 2008). Again we can conclude, therefore, that the Scottish approach to citizenship and education for citizenship operates more at the social than the political end of the citizenship spectrum.

WHAT KIND OF CITIZEN? WHAT KIND OF DEMOCRACY?

In the previous sections I have tried to characterise the particular take on citizenship and citizenship education that has been developed in Scotland over the past decade. The question I wish to address in this section focuses on the choices made or implied in this approach. After all, the idea of citizenship is itself not uncontested, and neither are views about the ways in which education might and can support citizenship. The question this raises, therefore, is what kind of citizenship is represented in the proposals, frameworks and inspection documents and, in relation to this, what kind of conception of democracy is pursued as a result of this – hence the title of this chapter. In order to do so, I will map the Scottish conception onto existing literature on citizenship and citizenship education. Before I do so, I wish to mention that there are remarkably few traces of philosophical or empirical literature in the framing documents for Scottish education for citizenship. As a result it is quite difficult to glance what has informed its authors, both in terms of their normative orientations and in terms of the empirical basis for their claims. Surely, it is not easy to come up with a framework for education for citizenship that can gain support across a broad political and ideological spectrum, which is often a reason why such documents are rather implicit about their normative orientations and political choices. Nonetheless there are real choices to be made – choices with important implications for educational practice and ultimate for the quality of citizenship and democratic life itself.

In order to locate the Scottish approach I will make use of a framework developed by Joel Westheimer and Joseph Kahne which they developed from their analysis of educational programmes for the promotion of democratic citizenship in the United States (see Westheimer & Kahne, 2004). Westheimer and Kahne make a distinction between three visions of citizenship that they found as answers to the question "*What kind of citizen do we need to support an effective democratic society*" (ibid., p. 239). They refer to these as the *personally responsible citizen*; the *participatory citizen*; and the *justice-oriented citizen*. Westheimer and Kahne claim that each of these visions of citizenship "reflects a relatively distinct set of theoretical and curricular goals" (ibid., p. 241). They emphasise that these visions are *not* cumulative. "Programs that promote justice-oriented citizens do not necessarily promote personal responsibility or participatory citizenship." (ibid.) What, then, characterises each of these visions of citizenship?

The *personally responsible citizen* "acts responsibly in his or her community by, for example, picking up litter, giving blood, recycling, obeying laws, and staying out of debt. The personally responsible citizen contributes to food or clothing drives when asked and volunteers to help those less fortunate, whether in a soup kitchen or a senior centre. Programmes that seek to develop personally responsible citizens attempt to build character and personal responsibility by emphasizing honesty, integrity, self-discipline, and hard work" (ibid., p. 241).

Participatory citizens are those "who actively participate in civic affairs and the social life of the community at the local, state, or national level. (...) Proponents of this vision emphasize preparing students to engage in collective, community-based efforts. Educational programs designed to support the development of participatory citizens focus on teaching students how government and community-based organizations work and training them to plan and participate in organized efforts to care for people in need or, for example, to guide school policies. Skills associated with such collective endeavors – such as how to run a meeting – are also viewed as important (...). (P)roponents of participatory citizenship argue that civic participation transcends particular community problems or opportunities. It develops relationships, common understandings, trust and collective commitments [and thereby] adopts a broad notion of the political sphere" (ibid., pp. 241–242).

Justice-oriented citizenship – "the perspective that is least commonly pursued" (ibid., p. 242) – is based on the claim "that effective democratic citizens need opportunities to analyze and understand the interplay of social, economic and political forces" (ibid.). Westheimer and Kahne refer to this approach as 'justice-oriented' because advocates of this approach call explicit attention "to matters of injustice and to the importance of pursing social justice" (ibid.). "The vision of the justice-oriented citizen shares with the vision of the participatory citizen an emphasis on collective work related to the life and issues of the community. Its focus on responding to social problems and to structural critique make it somewhat different, however [as they seek] to prepare students to improve society by critically analyzing and addressing social issues and injustices. (...) These programmes are less likely to emphasize the need for charity and voluntarism as ends in themselves and more likely to teach about social movements and how to effect systemic change." (ibid.)

Westheimer and Kahne sum up the differences between the three approaches in the following way: "(I)f participatory citizens are organizing the food drive and personally responsible citizens are donating food, justice-oriented citizens are asking why people are hungry and acting on what they discover." (ibid.)

Although educators who aim to promote justice-oriented citizenship may well employ approaches that make political issues more explicit than those who emphasize personal responsibility or participatory citizenship, Westheimer and Kahne stress that "the focus on social change and social justice does not imply emphasis on particular political perspectives, conclusions, or priorities" (ibid., pp. 242–243. They do not aim "to impart a fixed set of truths or critiques regarding the structure of society" but rather "want students to consider collective strategies for change that challenge injustice and, when possible, address root causes of problems" (ibid., p. 243). From a democratic point of view it is fundamentally important that the process respects "the varied voices and priorities of citizens while considering the evidence of experts, the analysis of government leaders, or the particular preferences of a given group or of an individual leader" (ibid.). Thus "students must learn to weigh the varied opinions and arguments" and must develop "the ability to communicate with and learn from those who hold different perspectives" (ibid.).

When we look at the Scottish approach to education for citizenship against this background, it is obvious that there are elements of all three orientations. This, as I have shown, is particularly the case in the 2002 *Education for Citizenship* document although already within that document we can see a shift which is taken up, more explicitly in later documents – most notably in the HMIE *Education for Citizenship* paper – towards an emphasis on personal responsibility. What emerges from the analysis, so I wish to suggest, is that the conception of citizenship informing the Scottish approach is predominantly that of the personally responsible citizen. Within the documents there is also a strong emphasis on participation. Although this shifts the conception of citizenship towards a more participatory approach, I am inclined to understand this mainly in relation to the approach to educational processes aimed at promoting citizenship, than that they are central to the *conception* of citizenship pursued. It is, in other words, important to make a distinction between the conception of *citizenship* and the conception of citizenship *education* in the documents, and my suggestion is that the conception of citizenship veers more towards the personally responsible citizens, whereas participation is presented as a key dimension of how students can *become* such citizens. This is, of course, not all black and white, but I hope to have presented a sufficiently detailed reading of the documents to warrant this conclusion.

By mapping the Scottish approach onto the categories suggested by Westheimer and Kahne, it is possible to get a better understanding of the specific position presented in the documents analysed in this chapter. It makes it possible to see, in other words, that the Scottish approach represents a particular *choice*, and that other options are possible. As such one could argue that this is all that can be said, as this is how education for citizenship in Scotland is conceived. But the further question that can be asked is whether the choice presented in the Scottish approach is the 'best' choice. Answering this question all depends on how one wishes education for citizenship to function and, most importantly, in what way and to what extent one wishes education for citizenship to contribute to a particular – democratic – con-figuration of society. At this point I wish to briefly discuss some of the concerns expressed by Westheimer and Kahne about the first conception of citizenship in their model, that of the personally responsible citizen which, according to them, is actually the most popular approach (see ibid., p. 243).

Westheimer and Kahne make it clear that in their view the emphasis on personal responsibility in citizenship is "an inadequate response to the challenges of educating a democratic citizenry" (ibid.) Critics of the idea of the personally responsible citizen have noted "that the emphasis placed on individual character and behavior obscures the need for collective and public sector initiatives; that this emphasis distracts attention from analysis of the causes of social problems and from systematic solutions" and that "voluntarism and kindness are put forward as ways of avoiding politics and policy" (ibid.) The main problem Westheimer and Kahne see is that whilst no one "wants young people to lie, cheat, or steal" the values implied in the notion of the personally responsible citizen "can be at odds with democratic goals" (ibid.). "(E)ven the widely accepted goals – fostering honesty, good neighborliness, and so on – are not *inherently* about democracy" (ibid.; emphasis in original) To put it differently: while many of the values and traits enlisted in relation to the personally responsible citizen "are desirable traits for people living in a community (...) they are not about democratic citizenship" (ibid.). And, even more strongly: "To the extent that emphasis on these character traits detracts from other important democratic priorities, it may actually hinder rather than make possible democratic participation and change." (ibid.). To support their point, Westheimer and Kahne report on research that found that fewer than 32% of eligible voters between the ages of 18 and 24 voted in the 1996 presidential election, but that "a whopping 94% of those aged 15–24 believed that 'the most important thing I can do as a citizen is to help others'" (ibid.). In a very real sense, then, "youth seems to be 'learning' that citizenship does not require democratic governments, politics, and even collective endeavours" (ibid.).

CONCLUSIONS

The main problem, therefore – and I have hinted at this already in passing – is that a too strong emphasis on personal responsibility, on individual capacities and abilities, and on personal values, dispositions and attitudes not only runs the risk of *depoliticising* citizenship by seeing it mainly as a personal and social phenomenon. It also runs the risk of not doing enough to empower young people as *political* actors who have an understanding both of the opportunities and the limitations of individual political action, and who are aware that real change – change that affects structures rather than operations within existing structures – often requires collective action and initiatives from other bodies, including the state. To quote Westheimer and Kahne once more: the individualistic conception of personally responsible citizenship rarely raises questions about "corporate responsibility ... or about ways that government policies can advance or hinder solutions to social problems" and therefore tends to ignore "important influences such as social movements and government policy on efforts to improve society" (ibid., p. 244). An exclusive emphasis on personally responsible citizenship "apart from analysis of social, political, and economic contexts" may therefore well be "inadequate for advancing democracy" as there is "nothing inherently *democratic* about personally responsible citizenship" and, perhaps even more importantly, "undemocratic practices are sometimes associated with programs that rely exclusively on notions of personal responsibility" (ibid., p. 248; emphasis in original).

This, then, is the risk that comes with a conception of citizenship and citizenship education that focuses too strongly on individual responsibility and individual traits, values and dispositions. While the Scottish approach is definitely not one-dimensional, and while what happens in the practice of education covers a much wider spectrum of possibilities, the available frameworks for understanding and promoting citizenship in and through education raise concern and could do with more attention for the political dimensions of citizenship and the promotion of forms of political literacy that position democratic citizenship beyond individual responsibility. Such an approach, as I have suggested in this chapter, does imply a particular, more political conception of citizenship but does not require a particular party-political choice. In this respect a broad consensus about education for citizenship can also be built around a view in which citizenship is more explicitly connected with wider social and political action and with a view of democracy as requiring more than just active, committed and responsible citizens.

3

European Citizenship and Higher Education

Whereas much discussion about citizenship and citizenship education has taken place within the confines of the nation state, the development of the European Union has added a new dimension. In this chapter I discuss the rise of the idea of European citizenship, particularly in relation to European higher education policy and research. This will not only allow me to highlight the specific character of these discussion and developments but also to indicate where national and supra-national thinking about citizenship, education and lifelong learning appears to converge. The European case also provides an example of a strong connection between research and policy, which raises important questions about the position of research in this field.

EUROPEAN CITIZENSHIP

Although the notion of European citizenship was already introduced in the Maastricht Treaty in 1992, there have been ongoing discussions about the shape and form of European citizenship. At stake in these discussions are normative questions about what European citizenship should look like and empirical questions about the kinds of citizenship that are actually emerging within and across the member states of the European Union. A key question in this regard is whether the European Union is best understood as a problem-solving entity based on economic citizenship, a rights-based post-national union, based on political citizenship, a value-based community premised on social and cultural citizenship, or as a particular combination of these dimensions.

A specific problem for the development and enhancement of European citizenship lies in the fact that citizenship is commonly experienced at a national level. This is not only because the nation state is the original guarantor of citizenship rights. It is also because there are more opportunities for citizens to identify with and participate in democratic processes and practices at local, regional and, to a certain extent, national level than that there are in relation to something as remote and abstract as the European Union. This partly explains why European citizenship has predominantly developed along economic lines, since for many inhabitants of the European Union the impact of the Union – both positively and negatively – is most strongly experienced in the economic domain, for example in relation to employment, economic legislation, the single currency and regional development. Historically this is also where the origins of the idea of European citizenship can be found, as the idea of European citizenship first of all emerged in the context of the question of free movement of economically active persons. In the Treaty of Paris (1951) this was restricted to workers in the European coal and steel industries. In the Treaty of Rome (1957) it was extended to all workers and services. Eventually this developed into a general right "of free movement and residence throughout the Union." Compared to the economic dimension, the socio-cultural and political dimensions, which have to do with the extent to which inhabitants of the member states see themselves as European citizens and identify with and actively support the European Union as a unit of democratic governance, are far less developed. Results from Eurobarometer 69 (Spring, 2008) indicate, for example, that just over half of those polled (52%) believe that membership of the European Union is a good thing, that 54% believe that their country has benefited from membership, and that 50% tend to trust the European Union (compared to only 34% who trust their National Parliament and 32% who trust their National Government). Moreover, there are significant differences between the different member states and between different segments of society within each member state, and on several indicators a downwards trend seems to have set in recently (see European Commission, June 2008).

The most prominent policy development in relation to the socio-cultural and political dimensions lies in the promotion of what is known as 'active citizenship' (see Benn, 2000; Wildermeersch, Stroobants & Bron, 2005). Within official European policy the idea of active citizenship first emerged in the context of the Lisbon European Council in March 2000. Here the strategic goal was set for the European Community to become "the most competitive and dynamic knowledge-based economy in the world with more and better jobs and greater social cohesion" (Lisbon European Council, 2000). In the communication Making a European area of lifelong learning a reality the European Commission promoted three major pillars, one of which was 'learning for active citizenship' (see European Commission, November 2001). In the Detailed work programme on the follow-up of education and training systems in Europe (Education Council, 2002), the European Council formulated 13 objectives related to the Lisbon programme. Objective 2.3 was "supporting active citizenship, equal opportunities and social cohesion" (see De Weerd et al., 2005, p. 1). In the wake of this much effort has been invested in developing indicators and instruments for measuring active citizenship (see Hoskins et al., 2006; Hoskins et al., 2008; Holford, 2008), thus making the idea of active citizenship a central plank in the European Union's approach to the development of citizenship.

While compulsory education has largely remained tied to national priorities (albeit with increasing efforts to include 'a European dimension' in its curricula), higher education is rapidly evolving into a sector that transcends national borders and agendas. The 'Europeanisation' of higher education is partly the result of long-standing exchange programmes such as the Erasmus programme (which celebrated its 20th anniversary in 2007). The main impetus for the transformation of European higher education, however, has come from a series of policy initiatives aimed at the creation of a European Higher Education Area (Bologna Declaration, 1999), a European Research Area (European Commission, January 2000), and a European Area of Lifelong Learning (European Commission, November 2001). The Lisbon Strategy has been a major driver behind these initiatives. Although the economic imperative is central in this strategy (see also chapter 5) – and has become even more central in the 2005 relaunch of the Lisbon Strategy with its explicit focus on "growth and jobs" – policy makers are aware of the wider potential of higher education in relation to questions of social cohesion and European citizenship (see European Commission, 2003; 2005; 2006; London Communiqué, 2007; see also Zgaga, 2007, pp. 99–111). This potential has also been emphasised by representatives from European higher education institutions, who have stressed that their role encompasses more than only the creation of the next generation of workers for the knowledge economy, but that it includes a responsibility for cultural, social and civic development at national and European level (see EUA, 2002; 2003; 2005; see also Simons, Haverhals & Biesta, 2007).

The question this raises is what kind of citizenship might be promoted in and through European higher education and also what kind of processes – educational and otherwise – might contribute to this. What, in other words, is the particular potential of European higher education for the development of European citizenship? To ask the question in this way suggests a rather straightforward framing in which it is assumed that it is clear what kind of citizenship is desirable for Europe so that the only questions with regard to European higher education have to do with the particular curricula, pedagogies and extra-curricular activities that might contribute to the development of this kind of citizenship. There is indeed a strong tendency within policy and research to frame the question in this way (see, for example, Fernández, 2005) and, more specifically, to ask how European higher education can and does contribute to the development of the competences necessary for active citizenship (see Hoskins, D'Hombres & Campell, 2008; Hoskins & Mascherini, 2009). In what follows I wish to question this particular framing. On the one hand I wish to challenge the near hegemony of the idea of active citizenship by raising some critical questions about this particular construction of citizenship and the underlying notion of democracy. On the other hand I wish to problematise the conception of political education and civic learning implied in the idea of civic competence. My intention is not to dismiss all the work that has been done in this area. I rather want to highlight the choices implied in the particular constructions of citizenship and civic learning at stake, so as to be able to expose the limitations of the prevailing view so that alternative constructions and configurations can be considered. As I will argue in more detail below, I am particularly concerned about three issues: (1) the de-politicising tendencies in the idea of active citizenship; (2) a too strong emphasis on consensus in the underlying conception of democracy; and (3) the reduction of citizenship education and civic learning to forms of socialisation. The question this raises, then, is whether European higher education should become one more socialising agent for the production of the competent active citizen, or whether there could and should be a more critical role for higher education in relation to European citizenship.

ACTIVE CITIZENSHIP AND ITS LIMITS

The main discourse that has emerged in the context of European citizenship is that of 'active citizenship.' The key-idea of active citizenship is that of participation. In the project on 'Active Citizenship for Democracy' (Hoskins, 2006), active citizenship for democracy was defined as "participation in civil society, community and/or political life, characterised by mutual respect and non-violence and in accordance with human rights and democracy" (Hoskins, 2006, quoted in Hoskins et al., 2006, p. 10).

De Weerd *et al.* (2005, p. ii), define active citizenship as "political participation and participation in associational life characterized by tolerance and non-violence and the acknowledgement of the rule of law and human rights." Associational life refers to "all associations and networks between family and the state in which membership and activities are voluntary" (ibid.). Active citizenship is therefore first and foremost about participation in civil society (see ibid.). De Weerd *et al.* (2005, p. ii) emphasise that the notion of active citizenship that should be promoted according to EU policy is not neutral but is characterized by the values of "tolerance [and] non-violence" and by "the acknowledgement of the rule of law and of human rights."

Hoskins *et al.* (2006, p. 9) locate the idea of active citizenship within the wider discussion about social capital, quoting Putnam's claim that active citizenship is "strongly related to 'civic engagement' and that it plays a crucial role in building social capital." According to Hoskins *et al.* (2006, p. 10) active citizenship is "partly overlapping with the concept of social values" and is a phenomenon that is mainly located at micro- and meso-level, that is, the "horizontal networks of households, individual households, and the associated norms and values that underlie these networks" and the "horizontal and vertical relations among groups." Active citizenship is explicitly not restricted to the political dimensions. Rather, "(i)t ranges from cultural and political to environmental activities, on local, regional, national, European and international levels [and] includes new and less conventional forms of active citizenship, such as one-off issue politics and responsible consumption, as well as the more traditional forms of voting and membership in parties and NGOs" (ibid., p. 11). The limits of active citizenship, according to Hoskins *et al.* (2006, p. 11) "are set by ethical boundaries," which means that people's activities "should support the community and should not contravene principles of human rights and the rule of law." This means that participation "in extremist groups that promote intolerance and violence should therefore not be included in this definition of active citizenship" (ibid.; see also Hoskins & Mascherini, 2009, p. 462.).

Work on the development of indicators for active citizenship so that active citizenship can be measured, has focused on four dimensions of active citizenship that together constitute the Active Citizenship Composite Indicator (ACCI). These are: "participation in political life, civil society, community life and the values needed for active citizenship (recognition of the importance of human rights, democracy and intercultural understanding)" (Hoskins *et al.*, 2006, p. 11). Participation in political life "refers to the sphere of the state and conventional representative democracy such as participation in voting, representation of women in the national parliament and regular party work (party membership, volunteering, participating in party activities and donating money)" (ibid., p. 12). Participation in civil society refers to "political non-governmental action" (ibid.). This dimension is based on 18 indicators with the sub-dimensions of "protest, human rights organisations, environmental organisations and trade union organisations" (ibid.). Participation in community life refers to activities "that are less overtly political and more orientated towards the community – 'community-minded' or 'community-spirited' activities" (ibid.). What distinguishes these activities from participation in civil society is that they are "more orientated towards community support mechanisms and less towards political action and accountability of governments" (ibid., p. 13). There are seven sub-dimensions under this dimension, namely "unorganised help, religious organisations, business organisations, sport organisations, cultural organisations, social organisations, [and] parent-teacher organisations" (ibid.). In each case the indicators look at membership, participation, donating money, and voluntary work. The indicators for values are sub-divided into democracy, human rights and intercultural competences (see ibid., p. 15). With regard to democracy the five indicators have to do with opinions about how important it is for a citizen to vote, to obey laws, to develop an independent opinion, to be active in a voluntary organisation, and to be active in politics (see ibid., p. 15).

In a further iteration of the Active Citizenship Composite Indicator (Hoskins & Mascherini, 2009) there is a slightly different set of indicators comprising protest and social change, community life, representative democracy and democratic values. 'Representative democracy' is a slightly more specific version of 'participation in political life' as it focuses on "voter turn out, participation in political parties and representation of women in parliament" (ibid., p. 466). 'Community life' covers the same areas as 'participation in community life' in the earlier version. 'Protest and social change' covers aspects of 'participation in civil society' with a particular emphasis on activities "to 'improve things' or 'prevent things from going wrong'" (ibid., p. 465) – which includes items such as "participating in a lawful demonstration, signing a petition, boycotting products and deliberately buying certain products" (ibid.), but also refers to "participation or volunteering activities organised by civil societies that work towards government accountability and positive social change" (ibid.). 'Democratic values' covers the same areas as 'indicators for values.'

Although the work on the development of indicators for active citizenship is primarily being conducted in order to measure levels of civic participation across the European Union, it is also a helpful source of information for gaining a better understanding of what active citizenship stands for and how it is being conceived and operationalised within the European policy context. This makes it possible to characterise the particular assumptions in the idea of active citizenship which, in turn, makes it possible to articulate what is and what is not included in the particular notion of citizenship put forward. With regard to this I wish to suggest that the idea of active citizenship as articulated in these documents is distinctive in three ways. Firstly it tends to be functionalistic; secondly it tends to be individualistic in that it focuses on the activities and responsibilities of individuals rather than activities of collectives or responsibilities of the state; thirdly, it tends to be based on a consensus rather than a conflict notion of democracy. I wish to emphasise that I speak of tendencies within the notion of active citizenship to emphasise particular aspects more than others. It is not, as I will make clear below, that other aspects are in all cases completely absent.

FUNCTIONALISM

To begin with the first point: the view of citizenship expressed in the idea of active citizenship denotes a set of activities which, as Hoskins, D'Hombres & Campbell (2008, p. 389) have put it, "are considered necessary for a stable democracy and social inclusion." They add that although active citizenship "is specified on the individual level in terms of actions and values, the emphasis in this concept is not on the benefit to the individual but on what these actions and values contribute to the wider society in terms of ensuring the continuation of democracy, good governance and social cohesion" (ibid.). This is one of the reasons why active citizenship is different from social capital as the reason for promoting active citizenship lies first and foremost in "assuring the democratic, human rights and social good at the country level" (Hoskins & Mascherini, 2009, p. 463). The concept of active citizenship thus "has much less of a focus on the benefit to the individual" (ibid.). The functionalist orientation of active citizenship also comes to the fore in relation to its role in social cohesion. Hoskins and Mascherini note that "(o)ne could hypothesise that the role of active citizens within social cohesion is to be the force involved in maintaining the values of equality and diversity through the activities of civil society" (ibid.). Yet the question this poses – and is posed by Hoskins and Mascherini – is to what extent "protests and unconventional forms of Active Citizenship [are] *allowed* within a socially cohesive society" (ibid., pp. 463–464; emphasis in original). The functionalist tendency is also visible in the 'community life' dimension which focuses on "participation in activities that support a community" (ibid., p. 465) and where being actively engaged in a community is seen as an indicator of active citizenship. Being 'in' a community is therefore considered to be more desirable than being 'outside' of a community – although it does of course matter what kind of community one is involved in. This is the reason why the active citizenship indicator also has a values dimension as this specifies the particular values that should underpin participation in community life and community life itself.

All this suggest that the idea of active citizenship approaches the idea of citizenship very much from the 'needs' of the socio-political order. It specifies the kinds of activities and 'investments' that individuals need to make so that the specific socio-political order can be reproduced. Active citizenship, to put it differently, emphasises the duties and responsibilities of individuals that come with their status of citizenship more than that it is a discourse about citizenship rights. One could, of course, argue that the two complement each other, but it is important to acknowledge that the idea of active citizenship mainly emphasises one side of the citizenship 'settlement' and has very little to say about the rights dimension.

There are two further points to be made in relation to this. Firstly, it could be argued that the relationship between citizenship rights and citizenship duties and responsibilities should be seen as a reciprocal one. One could argue that citizenship rights can only be guaranteed if there is sufficient (active) support from citizens for structures and practices of governance and the law. Yet this would provide an even stronger reason for a broader notion of citizenship than one which emphasises just one part of the citizenship settlement. What also should not be forgotten is the specific political history of the idea of active citizenship, at least in the Anglo-American context (as discussed in chapter 1).

INDIVIDUALISM

This also helps to explain the second characteristic of the idea of active citizenship, which is the tendency to emphasise the activities of *individuals*, that is, their ability and willingness to participate actively in civil society, and social and community and political life, rather than to focus on collective action or the responsibilities of the state. Hoskins and Mascherini do indeed acknowledge that active citizenship highlights a "shift towards examination of individual action" (Hoskins & Mascherini, 2009 p. 461). While there may be good reasons for highlighting the contribution of individuals, the individualisation of citizenship becomes a problem if it becomes the sole foundation for effective political action. This is a point most forcefully made by Zygmunt Bauman in his *In Search of Politics* (1999). In this book Bauman argues that what our post- or 'liquid' modern society seems to have lost are spaces, places and opportunities where 'private worries' can be translated into 'public issues' (see Bauman, 1999, p. 2). These are spaces "where private problems meet in a meaningful way – that is, not just to draw narcissistic pleasures or in search of some therapy through public display, but to seek collectively managed levers powerful enough to lift individuals from their privately suffered misery" (ibid., p. 3). The key question here is whether active citizenship always starts from private motivations – a form of citizenship which Bauman refers to as 'consumerist' (ibid., p. 4) – or whether citizenship or, more specifically, *democratic* citizenship, is actually motivated by a concern for the common good even if this were to require 'self-limitation' (see ibid.; see also Biesta, 2004[a]). Although active citizenship places a strong emphasis on participation, the question is, in other words, whether participation is understood as a *political* process – in which case participation involves the translation of private worries into collective issues – or whether it is understood in *consumerist* terms – in which case collective action would be nothing more than the aggregation of individual preferences. The operationalisation of the idea of active citizenship does pay attention to representative democracy and democratic values but says relatively little about the content of such processes and in this respect does locate the responsibility and motivation for participation first and foremost with the individual.

This relates to a second problem with the individualistic tendency in the idea of active citizenship which has to do with the question of the resourcing of civic action. Civic action, after all, does not simply depend on what individuals decide to do or not to do; it also crucially depends on the opportunities they have for participation. Again, the work on indicators acknowledges that such things as access to (public) transport do impact on the extent to which citizens can actively participate. The more fundamental question here, however, is whether societies – and in the case of European citizenship, the European Union as whole – see it as their responsibility to make resources available for active citizenship or whether this mostly depends on individual initiative. This is particularly an issue for the field of adult education which historically has been one of the places in society that allowed for the development of an understanding of how structural processes impact on private problems and opportunities and that provided opportunities for the translation of 'private worries' into 'collective issues' (see, for example, Martin, 2002; Fieldhouse, 1996). Support for adult education is therefore an important investment in civil society with crucial spin offs for the quality of political life. But as I will discuss in more detail in chapters 5 and 6, in many Western countries adult education has become reduced to only one of its functions, namely that of employability or 'learning for earning.' Any other forms of adult education – particularly those with potential political and politicising significance – have become (almost) completely dependent on the willingness of individuals to invest in their own education.

The functionalist and individualist tendencies within the idea of active citizenship both locate active citizenship more towards the social than towards the political end of the citizenship spectrum and thus show a strong convergence with the way in which citizenship is conceived and approach in the Scottish Curriculum for Excellence (as discussed in chapter 2). Although there is acknowledgement of the political dimensions of citizenship, there is a strong emphasis on activities that serve the needs of the community and society at large. What is far less emphasised is a notion of citizenship that is about collective political deliberation, contestation and action. This is why the idea of active citizenship runs the risk of de-politicising the very idea of citizenship itself. This risk is also reflected in the underlying conception of democracy.

DEMOCRACY AS CONSENSUS

The third distinguishing characteristic of the idea of active citizenship has to do with the underlying notion of democracy. The tendency within the idea of active citizenship is to see democracy in terms of consensus rather than in terms of plurality, disagreement and conflict. In the documents democracy is predominantly depicted as a value-based order. Active citizenship is not simply about *any* participation in civil society, community and/or political life but about participation "characterised by mutual respect and non-violence and in accordance with human rights and demo-cracy" (Hoskins, 2006, quoted in Hoskins *et al.*, 2006, p. 10). Hoskins emphasises, as I have shown, that the boundaries of active citizenship are of an *ethical* nature which means that people's activities "should support the community and should not contra-vene principles of human rights and the rule of law" (ibid., p. 11). Active citizens are those who subscribe to this order and actively contribute to its reproduction.

This line of thinking seems to hint at a consensus notion of democracy – and I say 'hint at' because the literature on active citizenship indicators actually says very little about underlying conceptions of democracy. Although there is a *prima facie* plausibility in the idea that a democratic society is based on certain values and that citizenship therefore entails support for such values, there is a deeper question about the justification of such values. This is, of course, first of all a question for political philosophy – but it is at the very same time a very practical question, particularly when the 'borders' of the democratic order are being challenged or contested. This is what Hoskins and Mascherini hint at when they ask to what extent protest and unconventional forms of active citizenship can be allowed within a socially cohesive society.

As I will discuss in more detail in chapter 7, there is a strong tendency within the literature, particularly as informed by liberal political philosophy, to see demo-cracy as a rational and moral order, that is, "the model which would be chosen by every rational individual in idealized conditions" (Mouffe, 2005, p. 121). On this account everyone who would challenge the democratic order would automatically have to be positioned on the other side of rationality, that is, either as irrational or, in case an educational perspective is taken, as pre-rational (see also Honig, 1993). Similarly, if the justification of the democratic order is conceived in moral terms – such as respect and tolerance – those who challenge the democratic order are automatically seen as immoral. This easily leads to a situation of 'us' and 'them' and labels those who challenge the particular democratic order as 'evil.' One of the practical disadvantages of such a positioning of those who are outside of the democratic order is that there is little basis for any meaningful exchange. This is one of the reasons why Chantal Mouffe has argued that we should understand the borders of the democratic order in strictly *political* terms, rather than in moral or natural terms. This not only allows for a different relationship between those who are 'inside' and those who are 'outside' – a point Mouffe has developed specifically in her earlier work (see Mouffe, 1993). It also allows for a contestation of the borders of the democratic order itself, rather than to assume that any currently existing democratic order is – perhaps even by definition – the ideal order.

This does not mean that Mouffe would advocate democracy without borders – or "pluralism without any frontiers" as she calls it (Mouffe, 2005, p. 120). She does not believe "that a democratic pluralist politics should consider as legitimate all the demands formulated in a given society" (ibid.). She argues that a democratic society "cannot treat those who put its basic institutions into question as legitimate adversaries" – but emphasises that exclusions should be envisaged "in political and not in moral terms" (ibid.). This means that when some demands are excluded, it is not because they are evil, "but because they challenge the institutions constitutive of the democratic political association" (ibid., p. 121). However – and this 'however' is crucial – for Mouffe "the very nature of those institutions" is also part of the debate. This is what she has in mind with her idea of 'conflictual consensus' which is a "consensus on the ethico-political values of liberty and equality for all, dissent about their interpretation" (ibid.). "A line should therefore be drawn between those who reject those values outright and those who, while accepting them, fight for conflicting interpretations." (ibid.) All this implies that for Mouffe "our allegiance to democratic values and institutions is not based on their superior rationality" which means that liberal democratic principles "can be defended only as being constitutive of our form of life" (ibid.) They are not the expression of a universal morality but are thoroughly 'ethico-political' (ibid.).

BEYOND THE ACTIVE CITIZEN

What these observations begin to reveal is not only that there are specific choices implied in the particular conception of active citizenship that is being pursued – and measured – within the European Union. They also hint at a different conception of active citizenship, one that is much more political and much more politicised and where the focus of civic activity is not simply on the reproduction of the existing democratic order but is also concerned about different interpretations and articulations of liberty, equality and democracy. Such a form of citizenship is less functional in relation to the existing order, is more driven by political and collective than

strictly individualistic concerns, and is more aware of the fact that different interpretations and articulations of the democratic values of liberty and equality point at
real alternatives. It would, therefore, be a form of citizenship which acknowledges
the possibility of a plurality of democratic settlements. Rather than aiming for one,
over-arching European conception of citizenship it would contribute to what Mouffe
describes as "an equilibrium among regional poles whose specific concerns and
traditions will be seen as valuable, and where different vernacular models of democracy will be accepted" (ibid., p. 129). Such a form of citizenship will no doubt be
active, but it hints at a different set of activities than those encapsulated by the
currently dominant notion of active citizenship. I return to this in chapter 7.

CIVIC COMPETENCE

The idea of 'active citizenship' is closely connected with a particular view on civic
learning and political education. The central idea in this view is that of 'civic competence.' The idea of competences emerged in European policy in the wake of the
Lisbon strategy. Whereas the language that was used originally was that of 'basic
skills,' this evolved over time into the language of 'competences.' Rychen (2004,
pp. 21–22) explains that skills "designate an ability to perform complex motor and/or
cognitive acts with ease and precision and an adaptability to changing conditions,"
whereas competence is a more holistic concept referring to "a complex action system
encompassing cognitive skills, attitudes and other non-cognitive components."
A competence thus refers to "a complex combination of knowledge, skills, understandings, values, attitudes and desires which lead to effective, embodied human
action in the world, in a particular domain" (Deakin Crick, 2008, p. 313). Activities
from a large number of working groups led to the formulation of the *European
Reference Framework of Key Competences for Lifelong Learning.* A version of this
was eventually adopted by the European Parliament in 2006 (European Council,
2006). It identified the following eight key competences (see Deakin Crick, 2008,
p. 312): communication in the mother tongue; communication in foreign languages;
mathematical competence and basic competences in science and technology; digital
competence; learning to learn; social and civic competences; sense of initiative and
entrepreneurship; and cultural awareness and expression. Within this framework
civic competence is conceived as the competence which "equips individuals to fully
participate in civic life, based on knowledge of social and political concepts and
structures and a commitment to active and democratic participation" (Education
Council, 2006, quoted in Hoskins, 2008, pp. 328–329).

Just as with the work on the measurement of active citizenship, it is the work on
the measurement of civic competence that provides most detail about how we should
understand civic competence and its constituting dimensions. In a recent report
Measuring Civic Competence in Europe (Hoskins *et al.*, 2008), civic competence is
defined as "the knowledge, skills, attitudes and values needed to enable individuals to
become an active citizen" (ibid., p. 11; see also pp. 22–23) and as "the ability required
for enabling individuals to become active citizens" (ibid., p. 13). More importantly for
the current discussion, civic competence is understood as a set of learning outcomes,

that is, as "the individual learning outcomes required for active citizenship" (ibid., p. 12). Whereas civic competence is characterised as the set of "individual outcomes" of relevant learning processes, active citizenship is seen as belonging to the "social outcomes" of civic competence (see ibid., p. 14). The literature thus gives the impression that civic competence is seen as a necessary but not a sufficient condition for active citizenship. Hoskins *et al.* write, for example, that "the ideal relationship between learning, civic competence and active citizenship" is one "where the learning develops certain civic competences that drive active citizenship" (ibid., p. 13). It is, however, only "in an ideal world" that civic competence translates into active citizenship as there may be "barriers that prevent young people who have the capacity for active citizens [sic] from participating" (ibid.).

The foregoing reveals that the acquisition of civic competence is seen as the key 'learning task' for the development of active citizenship. Although there may be 'barriers' that prevent the successful translation of civic competence into civic action, the idea is that *without* the possession of the specific set of knowledge, skills, attitudes and values that make up civic competence, no active citizenship will follow. Civic competence and active citizenship thus seamlessly hang together. This also means, however, that the problems related to the idea of active citizenship return in the idea of civic competence. The acquisition of civic competence is clearly meant to 'insert' individuals into the particular 'order' of active citizenship. In this regard the acquisition of civic competence is functionalistic. It is also individualistic. Civic learning, understood as the acquisition of civic competence is, after all, not depicted as a collective learning process, not as a process of collective politicisation and political contestation, but much more as an individual 'achievement.' It is the acquisition by the individual of the particular set of knowledge, skills, attitudes and values that are supposed to turn the individual into an active citizen, that is, the citizen who will contribute to the reproduction of the existing political order. It thus exemplifies what I wish to refer to as a *socialisation model* of civic learning and political education rather than a *subjectification model* of civic learning and political education. (I return to this distinction in chapter 7.) Whereas a socialisation model focuses on the 'insertion' of individuals into existing socio-political orders – and thus sees the purpose of civic learning and political education predominantly in terms of the reproduction of the existing order – a subjectification model is concerned with modes of civic learning and political education that support and promote political agency. The crucial question, therefore, is whether the idea of civic competence would allow for forms of civic learning that foster political agency and critical citizenship or whether its aim is mainly to 'domesticate' the citizen and channel his or her political agency into a very specific direction.

WHAT KIND OF CITIZENSHIP FOR EUROPEAN HIGHER EDUCATION?

In this chapter I have explored the question as to what kind of citizenship might be promoted in and through European higher education and how, through this, European higher education might contribute to the development of a truly European citizenship. Rather than providing a positive and programmatic answer to this question, I have analysed one possible framing of the issue, namely the one that argues that higher education should help individuals to acquire the competences they need in order to be or become active citizens. I have tried to argue that this is not just one possible answer amongst many to the question of the contribution of higher education to European citizenship, but that there is a strong tendency within policy and research to define European citizenship *as* active citizenship and to see civic and political learning for European citizenship in terms of the acquisition of the competences necessary for active citizenship. I have suggested that this is only one possible articulation of citizenship and civic learning and I have indicated some of the problems related to this particular framing of citizenship and learning. These problems have to do with de-politicising tendencies within the idea of active citizenship, a too strong emphasis on consensus in the underlying conception of democracy, and a reduction of civic learning to a form of socialisation aimed at the reproduction of the existing socio-political order (and it is interesting to see the strong convergence between these ideas and the ideas informing the understanding of citizenship in the Scottish Curriculum for Excellence as discussed in the previous chapter). Against this background I have argued for an understanding of citizenship that is more political than social, more concerned about collective than individual learning, that acknowledges the role of conflict and contestation, and that is less aimed at integration and reproduction of the existing order but also allows for forms of political agency that question the particular construction of the political order. I will return to these ideas in chapter 7. The underlying intuition here is that citizenship should first and foremost be seen as a *public* and a *political* identity and not as an individual and social one. This is why the individualisation and 'domestication' of citizenship runs the risk of undermining rather than promoting citizenship and civic action. There is, therefore a real choice for European higher education. It can either become one more socialising agent for the (re)production of the competent active citizen, or it can seek to support modes of political action and civic learning that embody a commitment to a more critical and more political form of European citizenship.

4

Knowledge, Democracy and Higher Education

In the previous chapter I have focused on the role of Higher Education in the promotion of citizenship, particularly through the lens of European citizenship. In this chapter I look once more at Higher Education, but now in more general terms, asking the question how Higher Education as a specific institution in society might contribute to democratisation and democratic citizenship. I am interested, in other words, in how we might understand the civic role and responsibility of Higher Education. Whereas in many countries around the world there is a strong emphasis on the potential contribution of Higher Education to the so-called knowledge economy, I introduce the idea of the 'knowledge democracy' in order to highlight the potential contribution of Higher Education to the democratisation of knowledge in society.

THE CIVIC ROLE OF HIGHER EDUCATION

The landscape of Higher Education in Europe is going through a period of rapid change. In many countries the Higher Education sector has come under an economic spell, expressed in the idea that the prime function of Higher Education is the training of a high-skilled workforce and the production of high quality scientific knowledge. According to European policy makers Universities should serve the knowledge society through the "production, transmission and dissemination" of high-quality knowledge (see Simons, 2006, p. 33). Higher Education has, of course, always been involved in the education of professionals and in research and development. What is new about the current situation is the changed context in which Universities have to operate. Whereas in industrial societies there existed an *indirect* relationship between knowledge production and the economy (the link was established through the industrial application of scientific knowledge and technology), in post-industrial societies knowledge has become an economic force in its own right (see Delanty, 2003). The fact that Higher Education has itself become a commodity in the global education market is but one example of this. As a result of these developments Higher Education has gained a much more prominent position in discussions about the future of the European economy and has become an explicit target of European policy makers (see Fredriksson, 2003). Initiatives such as the creation of the *European Research Area* (Lisbon, 2000) and the *European Area of Higher Education* (the 'Bologna Process') are part of a deliberate strategy to make Europe "the most competitive and dynamic knowledge based economy in the world, capable of sustained economic growth with more and better jobs and greater social cohesion" (Presidency Conclusions, Lisbon European Council, 23/24 March 2000).

Although there is no reason to doubt the economic importance of Higher Education, it is important to acknowledge that the role of the University is not exhausted by its economic function. There is, for example, a long-standing tradition in which it is argued that the University should be a place devoted to enquiry and scholarship free from any utilitarian demands. And although neo-liberal policies increasingly present a University education as an investment in one's future employability, we also should not forget those who engage in Higher Education first and foremost for personal fulfilment and for the intrinsic rather than the exchange value of a University degree. The question that I am interested in for this chapter, however, is not about the economic, scientific or personal function of Higher Education, but about the *civic* role of the University, that is, its particular role in democratic societies. I am interested, in other words, in the contribution Universities might be able make to the quality of democratic life and democratic processes. The purpose of this chapter is to explore the extent to which the contemporary University can still play such a role given the increased prominence of an economic discourse about its role, function and future. More importantly, I wish to examine *how* the contemporary University might perform its civic role and, through this, might contribute to processes of democratisation.

In what follows I will argue that the modern University can no longer lay claim to a 'research monopoly' since nowadays research is carried out in many places outside of the University. The University can, however, still lay claim to a kind of 'knowledge monopoly' which has to do with the fact that Universities still play an important role in the definition of what counts as 'scientific' knowledge, both through its research activities and, maybe even more importantly, through its teaching and its degree-awarding powers. (I use 'scientific' here in the broad sense akin to the German concept of 'wissenschaftlich,' which means that it encompasses the natural and social sciences and the humanities.) The problem is, however, that the University's knowledge monopoly is commonly understood and justified in *epistemological* terms. Whereas this only allows for one particular role of the University in a democratic society – namely, that of the expert – I will suggest a different way to understand the practice of the 'production, transmission and dissemination' of scientific knowledge. Against this background I will argue that there are two possible interpretations of the idea of the knowledge society, one called the *knowledge economy* and one called the *knowledge democracy.* My conclusion will be that the civic role of the University should particularly be connected to furthering the cause of the knowledge democracy. I will begin, however, with a brief overview of ideas about the civic role of the University.

HIGHER EDUCATION AND DEMOCRACY

The idea that Higher Education has a role to play in the maintenance and development of democratic societies is, as such, not new. Wilhelm von Humboldt's reinvention of the University in early nineteenth century Germany was closely related to the development of the German nation-state and to the formation (*Bildung*) of 'enlightened citizens' (see also Haverhals, 2007). Von Humboldt argued for a University informed by an ethos of 'Wissenschaftlichkeit' (scholarship), an ethos orientated towards the pursuit of truth understood as "the grasping of reality in its totality" (Simons, 2006, p. 38). For Von Humboldt the pursuit of truth was not exclusively a concern for academics. He believed that the exposition to and participation in processes that lead to the discovery of truth would cultivate a universal rationality in academics and students alike. He thus assumed that participation in the pursuit of truth was in itself a process of edification. Although Von Humboldt argued for a University free from external intervention, he did not believe that this would result in a University disconnected from wider social and political concerns. He maintained that the pursuit of truth would result in the enlightenment of the individual, society, the state, and mankind as a whole (see Simons, 2006, p. 39). In this way the pursuit of truth was to have individual and political significance at the very same time.

More than 100 years later Robert Maynard Hutchins, fifth president of the University of Chicago (from 1929–1945), articulated quite similar ideas. In his reflections on the purpose and form of Higher Education Hutchins made a strong case for a general, humanistic curriculum; a curriculum that would introduce all University students to the main intellectual achievements of Western civilisation (see Hutchins, 1936). He advocated an undergraduate curriculum based on "a course of study consisting of the greatest books of the western world and the arts of reading, writing, thinking, and speaking, together with mathematics, the best exemplar of the processes of human reason" (Hutchins, 1936, p. 38). Whereas he felt that the modern specialist was cut off from every field but his own, Hutchins believed that a liberal arts college experience could provide a basic shared intellectual experience. Such an education would bring about intellectual discipline, an appreciation of the good life and a capacity for judgement, which he considered to be of crucial importance for the participation of informed citizens in democratic life (see also Oelkers, 2005, pp. 31–32).

The idea that Higher Education's contribution to democracy lies first and foremost in the education of enlightened, informed and critical citizens, also plays a prominent role in more recent discussions about the role of Higher Education in democratic societies. In such discussions there is a strong emphasis on the importance of curricula and teaching practices that help students to develop a questioning and critical attitude (see, for example, Barnett, 1997; Rowland, 2003). Whereas some see the contribution of Higher Education specifically in the 'production' of a particular kind of critical citizen, others argue for the need of a transformation of Higher Education itself. Delanty (2003), for example, suggests that Universities should becomes sites of public discourse rather than sites of exclusive expertise, so that they can become "important agents of the public sphere, initiating social change rather than just responding to it" (Delanty, 2003, p. 81; see also Delanty, 2001). Giroux presents a similar view when he makes the case that Higher Education can and should function "as a vital public sphere for critical learning, ethical deliberation and civic engagement" (Giroux, 2003, p. 196).

What unites these suggestions is that they are all, in a sense, *normative*. They all specify a particular course of action, a particular educational and curricular 'programme' that needs to be instated and executed in order for Higher Education to perform its civic role. Although such normative approaches are, as such, not *un*-important since they may well have a positive impact on democracy and democratisation, they are not without problems either. One crucial problem stems from the fact that European Universities, unlike their North-American counterparts (see Trow, 1973; Fuller, 2003), are basically (still) *elite* institutions. They have a limited and also a quite specific 'reach.' Attempts to educate critical citizens through the University curriculum will therefore never reach the masses. Some might argue that there is no need to reach the masses as long as the elites – the future rulers – receive a proper democratic education. Yet it is not difficult to see that such a view goes directly against the principles of democracy. Others have spent much time and energy to actually widen the reach of the University. Here we can think, for example, of the University extension movement in the UK, the 'Volksuniversiteit' (People's University) in the Netherlands, Open Universities and more recent attempts to access to and participation in Higher Education.

The question, however, is not only how Universities can reach more people and how more people can benefit from a University education. The question that also needs to be addressed – and in a sense needs to be asked first – is what is special and even unique about the University *vis-à-vis* its civic role. What is it, in other words, that the University might contribute to democracy and democratisation and to the quality of democratic life that cannot be provided by any other institution or sector in society?

WHAT IS UNIQUE ABOUT THE UNIVERSITY?

Some argue that what is special about the University is the fact that it is a site for the conduct of research. But do Universities have a *research monopoly*? Are Universities the only places in society in which research is conducted? While this may be true for some fields of academic research, the general picture is that a substantial amount of research, both in the natural and the social sciences, is nowadays conducted outside of the University, often, but not exclusively in a commercial context. Universities find themselves increasingly competing on this 'research market' rather than that they occupy a unique or privileged position within it. This is, of course, not to deny that Universities are by and large places where research is one of the key-activities (although in the ever-expanding Higher Education sector there are more and more institutions that focus mainly on teaching), but we cannot claim that Universities are the only places where research is conducted.

If Universities do not have a research monopoly, could it be the case that they have a *knowledge monopoly*? Could it be the case that Universities produce a particular 'kind' of knowledge or knowledge of a particular 'quality'? This is, of course, an idea with a long-standing history and it has clearly informed Von Humboldt's view about the University and its civic role. There are also many more recent defenders of this idea. Whereas part of the discussion about the status of scientific knowledge focuses on the superiority of the scientific worldview compared to, for example, a religious understanding of reality (see, for example, Dawkins, 2006), a more compelling argument has been given by Ernest Gellner who has argued that it is the success of modern technology that proves the superiority of the scientific knowledge upon which it is based, and also proves the superiority of scientific rationality and the scientific worldview more generally (see Gellner, 1992). There are, however, also many who have questioned the special status of scientific knowledge and have pointed at the limits of the scientific worldview, both for our understanding of and for dealings with the natural and the social world (for a concise overview see Sardar, 2000).

If we were to take the strict view that Universities are indeed the producers of a special kind of knowledge, then the only civic role for the University becomes that of the *expert*, that is, the one who speaks with authority and whose arguments, because they are based on superior knowledge and informed by superior rationality, should, in principle, be given priority. Whether a case can be made for such a *de jure* knowledge monopoly remains to be seen, and I will return to this question below. I do believe, however, that *de facto* Universities do (still) play a crucial role in the definition of what counts as 'scientific' and what, in the wider society, is seen as 'scientific.' This has primarily to do with the fact that Universities have a monopoly on the education of researchers, particularly because they are the only institutions within the Higher Education sector with degree awarding powers. Through this Universities first of all control the definition of *who* counts as a qualified researcher. This, in turn, also contributes to the definition and perceived 'standard' of *what* counts as 'scientific'. This is not to suggest, of course, that the boundaries between 'science' and 'non-science' are clear and uncontested. I only wish to highlight the particular position that the University may have in relation to such boundary setting activities (see also Gieryn, 1983).

These considerations leave us with an interesting predicament. Whereas we cannot claim that the University has a research monopoly, a case can be made for the claim that it holds a knowledge monopoly. But when we interpret and justify this monopoly in epistemological terms, that is, by claiming that the University is the producer of a special kind of knowledge – more true, more real, more rational, etcetera – then the civic role of the University becomes confined to that of the expert. From a democratic point of view the problem with the expert position is that in the end it always overrules all other opinions. One may of course believe that this is what ultimately should happen, but in that case democracy becomes 'driven' by science – which in fact makes democracy superfluous. The more 'empirical' justification for the knowledge monopoly of the University – that is, the observation that the *de facto* Universities have an important role in the definition of what counts as scientific – does not lead to this problem, but raises the question to what extent the boundary setting activities of the University are merely arbitrary, something which again raises questions about democracy. And what is lurking in the background of these discussions is the 'technology argument,' that is, the suggestion that the technological 'success' of modern science both in the natural and the social sciences 'proves' the superiority, and hence the special quality of scientific knowledge.

In the next two sections I turn to the work of John Dewey and Bruno Latour. Their work provides a way of understanding the connections between knowledge production, democracy and the University that does not result in the either/or of science or democracy and that is also able to accommodate the technological success of modern social and natural science. Their work, as I will argue, hints at a quite different way to articulate the civic role of the University.

JOHN DEWEY AND THE CRISIS IN MODERN CULTURE

There is a widespread belief that John Dewey held modern science in high esteem and generally advocated the adoption of the scientific method in all fields of life. Because of this, some have accused Dewey of 'scientism', that is, the view that what the natural sciences have to say about the world is all there is to say. In his book *Eclipse of Reason* Max Horkheimer argued, for example, that Dewey's "worship of natural sciences" made it impossible for him to take a critical stance (see Horkheimer, 1947, pp. 46–49). Whereas Dewey was very clear about the value he attached to the scientific *method* because "its comparative maturity as a form of knowledge exemplifies so conspicuously the necessary place and function of experimentation" (Dewey, 1939, p. 12), he was equally clear in his view that his appreciation for the methods of the natural sciences "would be misinterpreted if it were taken to mean that science is the only valid kind of knowledge" (Dewey, 1929, p. 200). Dewey not only rejected the suggestion that the knowledge provided by the natural sciences is the only valid kind of knowledge. He even argued against the more general idea that knowledge is the only way in which we can get 'in touch' with reality. If there is one recurring theme in Dewey's work it is precisely his rejection of the idea that knowledge is the "measure of the reality of [all] other modes of experience" (ibid., p. 235).

According to Dewey the main problem of the identification of what is known with what is real, is that it makes it appear as if all other dimensions of human life – such as the practical, aesthetic, ethical, or the religious dimensions – can only be real if they can be reduced to and validated by what is revealed through our knowledge. By assuming that knowledge provides the 'norm' for what is real, other aspects of the ways in which human beings live their lives are relegated to the domain of the subjective: the domain of individual taste, points of view, feelings, and individual perspectives. As Dewey put it: "When real objects are identified ... with knowledge-objects, all affectional and volitional objects are inevitably excluded from the 'real' world, and are compelled to find refuge in the privacy of an experiencing subject or mind" (Dewey, 1925, p. 30). Dewey believed that the identification of what is known with what is real was one of the most fundamental mistakes of modern philosophy and referred to this mistake as the 'intellectualist fallacy' (Dewey, 1929, p. 175; see also 1925, pp. 28–30). Yet for Dewey this was not only a philosophical problem. It rather was a problem that lay at the heart of modern culture and that was central to what Dewey saw as a *crisis* in modern culture (see Dewey, 1939). In a sense Dewey's work can be read as a response to this crisis (see Biesta, 1992; Biesta & Burbules, 2003).

According to Dewey the crisis in modern culture is the result of the disintegrating effect of modern science on everyday life. Modern science has completely changed our understanding of the world in which we live. It has given us a view of the world as a mechanism, as "a scene of indifferent physical particles acting according to mathematical and mechanical laws" (Dewey, 1929, p. 33). Thus modern science "has stripped the world of the qualities which made it beautiful and congenial to men" (ibid.). According to Dewey, the disintegrative impact of this development on the world of everyday life is mainly caused by the way in which the scientific worldview has been interpreted, viz., as an accurate or 'true' account of reality as it really is. As we have already seen, this has led to the derogation of the reality of the world of everyday experience, and of the reality of the non-cognitive dimensions of human life.

> The net practical effect [of this interpretation of the scientific worldview] is the creation of the belief that science exists only in the things which are most remote from any significant human concern, so that as we approach social and moral question and interests we must either surrender hope of the guidance of genuine knowledge or else purchase scientific title and authority at the expense of all that is distinctly human. (Dewey, 1939, p. 51).

The problem is, in other words, that the realistic interpretation of the mechanistic worldview of modern science has put us in a situation in which there are two equally unattractive options: the 'inhuman rationality' of modern science or the 'human irrationality' of everyday life. This predicament lies at the hart of the crisis in culture, which means that this crisis should first and foremost be understood as a crisis of rationality.

The fact that Dewey relates the crisis in culture to a specific *interpretation* of the mechanistic worldview of modern science should not be read to imply that the crisis is only a theoretical problem and therefore has nothing to do with the urgent practical problems of contemporary life. Dewey rather wants to stress that the hegemony of scientific rationality and the scientific worldview   that is, the situation in which it is assumed that rationality only has to do with the 'hard facts' of science, and not with values, morals, feelings, emotions and so on – makes it almost impossible to find an adequate solution for these problems, since the situation we are in is one in which rationality gets restricted to facts and means, while values and ends are, by definition, excluded from rational deliberation. What makes all this even more urgent is the fact that to a large extent modern life is what it is as a result of the "embodiment of science in the common sense world" (Dewey, 1938[b], p. 81). We are, after all, constantly confronted by the products and effects of modern science, particularly through the omnipresence of technology in our lives, which seems to prove again and again the truth of the scientific worldview upon which it is based. This is why Dewey claimed that the world of everyday experience "is a house divided against itself" (Dewey, 1938[b], p. 84).

MODERN SCIENCE AND THE SPECTATOR VIEW OF KNOWLEDGE

The key question here is whether the interpretation of the scientific worldview as an account of what reality is really like, is inevitable. According to Dewey, this is not the case. His argument is partly philosophical and partly historical. The historical line of his argument focuses on the question why the scientific worldview has been interpreted as an account of what the world is really like. For this Dewey goes back to the birth of Western philosophy in Greek society. According to Dewey Western philosophy emerged in a society in which knowing was more valued than doing, and in which theory had a much higher status than practice (see Dewey, 1916, pp. 271–285). The reason for this hierarchy was a longing for absolute, immutable certainty and the recognition that such certainty could not be obtained in the domain of action (Dewey, 1929, pp. 5–6). The identification of what is certain with what is immutable led philosophers such as Plato to a metaphysics in which it was maintained that only what is fixed and unchangeable can be real, and to an epistemology in which it was argued that certain knowledge "must related to that which has antecedence existence or essential being" (Dewey, 1929, p. 18). One implication of this set of assumptions was that true knowledge could only be acquired if the process of acquisition did not exert any influence on the object of knowledge (see ibid., p. 19). For this reason the acquisition of knowledge was cut off from the domain of action and became understood in terms of visual perception – a theory that Dewey referred as the "spectator theory of knowledge" (ibid.). According to Dewey this has had a profound impact on our understanding of knowledge up to the present day. "(T)he notion which has ruled philosophy ever since the time of the Greeks, [is] that the office of knowledge is to uncover the antecedently real" (ibid., p. 14).

One of the interesting aspects of the Greek worldview was the assumption that values were part of reality. The Greeks assumed, in other words, that reality was purposeful. This meant that true, objective knowledge about reality would at the very same time provide us with guidelines for the direction of human action. It is not too difficult to see the kind of problems that arose when the mechanical worldview of modern science emerged. Whereas until then it had been possible to derive aims and values from our knowledge of the world, modern science "ceased to disclose in the objects of knowledge the possession of any such properties" (ibid., p. 34). This led to the question of how the results of the new science could be accepted and the domain of values maintained. Dewey argues that, given the available philosophical framework, that is, the spectator theory of knowledge, there appeared to be only one possible solution: values had to be relegated to a separate domain, the domain of the non-material, the spiritual and the subjective. To be able to accept the findings of modern science and safeguard the domain of values, philosophers such as Descartes and Kant thus introduced the distinction between mind and matter, between the objective and the subjective, and between facts and values. Whereas science was positioned at the side of matter, the objective and facts, all that was relevant for direction in the domain of human action ended up on the side of the mental and the subjective – and this created the framework in which the crisis in culture could emerge.

When, against this background, Dewey looks favourable at modern science it is first of all because his analysis shows that the road taken at the beginning of modern times, that is, to split mind and matter, the objective and the subjective, facts and values, was not inevitable but was only one of the available options.

Dewey argues that when modern science emerged there were *two* options for philosophy. The one that was taken was to use the existing philosophical framework to interpret the findings of modern science, and it was this 'move' that ultimately led to the crisis in modern culture. The road not taken, however, was to explore what would happen if we would adjust our theories of knowledge and reality in line with the findings and methods of modern science itself. It is the latter line which is central to Dewey's own understanding of knowing and knowledge.

DEWEY'S TRANSACTIONAL REALISM

Central to Dewey's approach is the idea that as living beings we are always already in interaction – or to use Dewey's notion: *transaction* – with the world. It is not that we first need to gain knowledge about the world before we can act. As living beings we are always already acting 'upon' and 'with' the world. As a result – and this is one of the key ideas of Dewey's 'transactional realism' (see Biesta & Burbules, 2003; Sleeper, 1986) – there is no longer a 'gap' between us and the world, unlike in the dualistic universe of modern philosophy. Transaction means that we are always 'in touch' with the world and this connection, in turn, ensures that our knowledge is always knowledge 'of' the world. The 'price' to pay for this – and this is the crucial element of Dewey's theory of knowing – is that we only know the world through our interactions with it. Unlike the spectator theory in which it was assumed that our knowledge is a picture of a world independent from us, Dewey's transactional realism implies that we only know the world *in function of* the ways in which we manipulate, interact with and intervene in the world. Our knowledge, in other words, is knowledge of the possible relationships between our actions and their consequences. We construct a world – or to be more precise: we construct objects of knowledge – on the basis of the perceived relationships between our actions and their consequences. The world and the objects within this world are therefore constructions. But they are not mental constructions; they are constructions that are based upon our transactions with the world, and in this respect they are real.

Dewey's transactional realism thus offers us a way to understand scientific (and everyday) knowledge as something that is 'of' the world but that, unlike in the spectator view of knowledge, is not 'objective.' One important advantage of this approach is that it allows us to accept the fact that knowledge can be useful in the form of technological applications, without having to accept the particular view of the world that is needed – constructed, as Dewey would say – in order to have successful technology. The world of atoms and genes is, in other words, not the ultimately real world; it is the world we construct on the basis of our transactions in order to do certain things, but it is no longer a world we have to accept as the one and only real and objective world. Dewey thus provides us with a way to interpret modern science and technology that does not force us to accept the scientific worldview as the one and only way to depict and understand the world. Interestingly enough he achieves this by taking modern science in its findings and its methods seriously.

Dewey's ideas have many ramifications for our discussion, not in the least because his depiction of the crisis in modern culture can also be seen as a crisis in democracy. The point, after all, is whether we have to accept the world of modern science as the one and only world, or whether we can see this world as one particular construction, fit for a particular purpose – the purpose of technology, so we might say – but not necessarily fit for all purposes. With Dewey the representatives of science can still be seen as experts, but their expertise is no longer epistemological – they are no longer experts of the one and only 'real' and objective world; instead, they are experts of particular ways to deal with and interact with the world. Dewey helps us to see, in other words, that the expertise of science is limited and situated. A further implication of Dewey's approach is that we can no longer understand the distinction between scientific knowledge and everyday knowledge itself in epistemological terms, that is, as a distinction between the objective knowledge of science and the subjective knowledge of the world of everyday life. The world of science and the world – or better: worlds – of everyday life have to be seen as different constructions, fit for different purposes. This means that – if we follow Dewey – we can no longer understand the knowledge monopoly of the University in epistemological terms, that is, in terms of the assumption that scientific knowledge is better, more true and more real that everyday knowledge and should therefore have prominence. This in itself already opens up important democratic questions around knowledge in our society and also opens up important democratic possibilities. It opens up a situation, in other words, in which we can legitimately raise questions about the relationships between different knowledges and views of the world, the scientific being one of them.

BRUNO LATOUR, TECHNO-SCIENCE AND METROLOGY

One author who has asked such questions – although not the only one who has done so (see Biagioli, 1999) – is the French 'anthropologist of science' Bruno Latour. Latour's work is relevant for my argument because in his studies of the role of 'techno-science' in modern society, he explicitly deals with what I have referred to above as the 'technology argument.' In the epistemological interpretation of techno-science it is assumed that 'techno-scientists' construct 'facts and machines' (Latour's phrase) in their laboratories which are then distributed to the world outside of the laboratory. The successful distribution of facts and machines to the wider world and, more importantly, the fact that facts and machines are able to 'survive' under non-laboratory conditions, is generally taken as a sign of the special quality of the knowledge underlying such facts and machines (see, for example, Gellner, 1992). What is interesting about Latour – and here there is a close connection with Dewey's approach (see also Biesta, 1992) – is that he sees no reason for doubting that techno-scientists are indeed able to create effective facts and machines in their laboratories. He also sees no reason to doubt that at a certain moment in time such facts and machines show up at other places than where they were originally constructed. But what Latour does challenge is the claim that what has happened in the mean time is a displacement of such facts and machines from the safe environment of the laboratory to the real world 'outside.' Latour argues that what in fact has happened is a displacement of the laboratory itself, that is, a displacement of the conditions under which facts and machines are able to exist and operate successfully. It is not that facts and machines have moved to a world outside of the laboratory. It is rather than the outside world has been transformed into a laboratory. As Latour writes:

No one has ever seen a laboratory fact move outside unless the lab is first brought to bear on an 'outside' situation and that situation is transformed so that it fits laboratory prescriptions. (Latour, 1983, p. 166).

Latour's work provides many fascinating examples of this process. In his book on Pasteur Latour argues, for example, that the success of Pasteur's approach was not the result of the displacement of a robust technique from Pasteur's laboratory to the farms in the French countryside. It could only happen because significant dimensions of French farms were transformed into a laboratory. They had to adopt the procedures of Pasteur's laboratory, in other words, before Pasteur's technique could be applied. It is, as Latour argues, "only on the conditions that you respect a limited set of laboratory practices [that] you can extend to every French farm a laboratory practice made at Pasteur's lab" (Latour, 1983, p. 152). What took place, therefore, was a 'Pasteurisation of France' (Latour, 1988). Latour refers to "this gigantic enterprise to make of the outside a world inside of which facts and machines can survive" as *metrology* (Latour, 1987, p. 251). Metrology can be understood as a process of creating 'landing strips' for facts and machines (ibid., p. 253). Metrology is a transformation of *society*, an incorporation of society into the network of techno-science, so that facts and machines can 'travel' without any visible effort. There is therefore, as Latour explains, "no outside of science but there are long, narrow networks that make possible the circulation of scientific facts" (Latour, 1983, p. 167).

Along these lines Latour thus criticises the main idea of the epistemological interpretation of the difference between scientific and everyday knowledge, which is that it is the alleged special quality of the knowledge invested in facts and machines that makes their universal displacement possible. Yet it is important to see that Latour does not simply reverse this argument. He does not say that it is the spreading of facts and machines that causes the knowledge invested in them to become universal (which would be a sociological interpretation of this phenomenon; for more detail see Biesta, 2002). The crux of Latour's analysis is that there is no displacement of facts and machines at all. They stay where they are. It is only because more and more 'points' (places, locations, people) become incorporated into a network that the illusion of movement arises. But in fact it is not that facts and machines move from the centre of the laboratory to the periphery of the real world. It rather is that the margins move towards, or become incorporated in the centre (and the identification of what is central and peripheral is, of course, itself an outcome of this).

This is of course not to suggest that there are no power differences between centre and margin, between strong and weak networks. With Latour we can see the world – the world which contains both scientific and everyday knowledge practices – as a collection of practices that, in a sense, are all local. Some of these practices, however, have been more successful in incorporating and transforming their 'outside' than others. This results in *asymmetry*, and one of the most striking asymmetries in modern societies – as we have also seen with Dewey – is the alleged asymmetry between science and everyday life and between scientific and everyday knowledge and rationality. Yet it is important to see that such asymmetries are not the outcome of qualitative, intrinsic or epistemological differences. Although there can be no doubt that there are qualitative differences between different practices, depending, among other things, upon the criteria that we use to evaluate them, such differences in quality do not in themselves cause asymmetries. Asymmetry, in Latour's vocabulary, only denotes that some networks are bigger, longer and stronger than others. What appears to be universal is, from this point of view, nothing more – but also nothing less – than an extension of a particular local practice. This does not say anything about the quality or value of such practices, although, as Latour argues, scientists themselves often try to define the asymmetries that they create in qualitative terms, such as 'knowledge' (*episteme*) versus 'belief' (*doxa*), 'scientific' versus 'common sense,' and even 'rational' versus 'irrational.' But apart from rhetorical gain – and there is, of course a lot to be gained by such rhetoric – there is no real point in doing this.

CONCLUSION: TOWARDS THE KNOWLEDGE DEMOCRACY

In this chapter I have explored the civic role of the University, by which I mean the contribution of Higher Education to the development and maintenance of democratic processes and practices. I have shown that the idea that the University has something to contribute to democracy and democratisation has a history that at least goes back to the Enlightenment and the emergence of the modern nation-state. A central tenet of this history is the idea that the University should focus on the education of enlightened, informed and critical citizens. This line of thinking also plays a prominent role in more recent exploration of the civic role of Higher Education. Although such strategies are not unimportant, I have argued that as long as the University remains an elite institution, it will only reach a small percentage of the population, which means that its impact on the citizenry will remain limited. I have therefore approached the question of the civic role of the University from a slightly different angle by asking what unique contribution the University might make to democracy and democratisation. I have argued that Higher Education can no longer lay claim to a research monopoly – since research is conducted in many places outside of the University – but it can still lay claim to a kind of knowledge monopoly, in that the University plays an important role in the definition of what counts as 'scientific' knowledge and what, in the wider society, is seen as 'scientific.' The key question is how we should interpret this knowledge monopoly. I have shown that there is (still) a strong tradition in which the knowledge monopoly of the University is understood in epistemological terms, that is, based on the assumption that the knowledge produced through scientific research is of a higher 'quality' – more true and more rational, for example – than the knowledge of everyday life. One important aspect of this line of argumentation is what I have referred to as the technology-argument, that is, the idea that the success of modern technology proves the superiority – and truth – of the scientific knowledge upon which technology is based. The problem with the epistemological interpretation of the knowledge-monopoly of the University is that it could undermine democracy. After all, the upshot of this interpretation is that only one way to see and understand the world is considered to be valid. I have used ideas from John Dewey to argue that it is possible to accept the success of modern technology without having to commit oneself to the scientific worldview. Dewey helps us to see, in other words, that scientific expertise is limited or, to be more precise, that it is *situated*. An important democratic 'gain' that follows from this approach is that it makes it possible to ask questions about the relationships between different knowledges and worldviews, the scientific worldview being one of them. Moreover, it allows us to explore how asymmetries between different knowledges and worldviews come into existence and are kept in place. It is the latter line of investigation which is central in the work of Latour. He provides an interesting way to understand the major asymmetry in modern society, namely the one between scientific and other forms of knowledge. Taken together, Dewey and Latour thus suggest an important agenda *vis-à-vis* the civic role of the University. Their work suggests that at least part of what Universities can contribute to democratisation lies in opening up the manifold ways in which scientific knowledge and technology are produced. Along these lines the University can make an important contribution to the democratisation of knowledge and can thus support the development of what I suggest to call the knowledge democracy. Whereas I do not want to suggest that the knowledge democracy should *replace* the knowledge economy – we must be realistic about the importance of techno-science for economic development – I do wish to suggest that we should see the knowledge democracy as one of the crucial dimensions of the knowledge society, so as to make sure that the knowledge society will never be reduced to the knowledge economy.

5

Lifelong Learning in the Knowledge Economy

The tension between economic and democratic imperatives is not only felt in schools, colleges and universities but is also increasingly having an impact on lifelong learning. In this chapter I review these developments and identify shifts and transformations in policy and practice. I show how the very definition of what lifelong learning is and what it is for has dramatically changed over the past decades, moving from a broad and encompassing conception of lifelong learning for economic, personal and political benefit towards a much more narrow view which emphasises first and foremost the economic rationale. This has gone hand in hand with an increased individualisation of lifelong learning – making lifelong learning the responsibility of individuals – and a shift from lifelong learning as a right individuals can claim towards lifelong learning as a duty that is put upon individuals in the name of such abstract ideals as 'the global economy' or 'global competitiveness.' I not only show how these shifts impact at the level of individuals but also make a case for the need to reconnect the idea of lifelong learning with the democratic imperative – an idea to which I refer as the 'learning democracy.'

FROM 'LEARNING TO BE' TO 'LEARNING TO BE PRODUCTIVE, EMPLOYABLE'

In 1972 UNESCO, the United Nations Educational, Scientific and Cultural Organisation, published a report written by the International Commission on the Development of Education under the chairmanship of Edgar Faure. Faure described the remit of his commission as "a critical reflection by men of different origins and background, seeking, in complete independence and objectivity, for over-all solutions to the major problems involved in the development of education in a changing universe" (Faure et al., 1972, p. v). The Commission did indeed only consist of men, but had an interesting international 'make up': Edgar Faure (France), former Prime Minister and Minister of Education; Professor Felipe Herrera (Chile), former President of the Inter-American Development Bank; Professor Abdul-Razzak Kaddoura (Syria), Professor of Nuclear Physics at the University of Damascus; Henri Lopes (People's Republic of Congo), Minister of Foreign Affairs, former Minister of Education; Professor Arthur V. Petrovsky (U.S.S.R.), Member of the Academy of Pedagogical Sciences of the U.S.S.R., Majid Rahnema (Iran), former Minister of Higher Education and Sciences; and Frederick Champion Ward (USA), Adviser on International Education, the Ford Foundation (see Faure et al., p. xi).

The report was titled *Learning to be: The world of education today and tomorrow*, and was hailed by the chairman of UNESCO, René Maheu, as "a global conception of education for tomorrow that [is] without doubt more complete than any formulated hitherto" (Faure *et al.*, 1972, p. ix). *Learning to be* made a strong case for lifelong education and for the development of a learning society. The authors of the report argued that in the world of today "studies can no longer constitute a definitive 'whole,' handed out to and received by the student before he embarks on adult life" since all that has to be learned "must be continually re-invented and renewed" (ibid., p. xxxiii). If, therefore, learning involves "all of one's life, in the sense of both time-span and diversity, and all of society" then, so the report concluded, we must go further than an overhaul of educational systems "until we reach the stage of a learning society" (ibid.).

Learning to be is a remarkable document for at least two reasons. On the one hand it is remarkable for the strength and breath of its vision about the role of education in the world. On the other hand *Learning to be* is remarkable as a historical document. This it not only because it reflects the world of the late sixties and early seventies so well, both in terms of its concerns and in terms of its optimism that change for the better was possible. But it is also because the views expressed in *Learning to be* about education and, more specifically, about lifelong education and the learning society, stand in such sharp contrast to the policies and practices that make up the world of lifelong learning today. Here, for example, is how Faure summarises the four basic assumptions of the report.

> The first ... is that of the existence of an international community which, amidst the variety of nations and cultures, of political options and degrees of development, is reflected in common aspirations, problems and trends, and in its movement towards one and the same destiny. The corollary to this is the fundamental solidarity of governments and of people, despite transitory differences and conflicts. The second is belief in democracy, conceived of as implying each man's right to realize his own potential and to share in the building of his own future. The keystone of democracy, so conceived, is education – not only education that is accessible to all, but education whose aims and methods have been thought out afresh. The third assumption is that the aim of development is the complete fulfilment of man, in all the richness of his personality, the complexity of his forms of expression and his various commitments – as individual, member of a family and a community, citizen and producer, inventor of techniques and creative dreamer. Our last assumption is that only an over-all, lifelong education can produce the kind of complete man the need for whom is increasing with the continually more stringent constraints tearing the individual asunder. We should no longer assiduously acquire know-ledge once and for all, but learn how to build up a continually evolving body of knowledge all through life – 'learn to be'. (Faure *et al.*, 1972, pp. v–vi)

To configure lifelong education in terms of solidarity, democracy and 'the complete fulfilment of man,' to contend that the aim of education is "*to enable man to be himself, to 'become himself'*" (ibid., p. xxxi, emph. in original), to argue that "*(w)ays of broadening and strengthening solidarity must be found*" (ibid., p. xxxviii, emph. in original), and even to suggest in a report on education the need for "the renunciation of nuclear weapons" (ibid., p. xxv), seems to be fundamentally different from the discourses, policies and practices of lifelong learning today.

I am not the first to comment on the fact that over the past two decades lifelong learning has increasingly come under the spell of an economic imperative, both at the level of policy and at the level of practice (see, for example, Edwards, 1997; Ranson, 1998; Boshier, 1998; Field, 2000; Fredriksson, 2003; Grace, 2004). A telling example at the level of European policy can be found in a speech by the Director-General of the General Directorate for Education and Culture of the European Commission (Van der Pas, 2001). After reminding his audience of the strategic goal of the European Union to make Europe "the most competitive and dynamic knowledge-based economy in the world" (p. 11; see also Lisbon European Council: Presidency Conclusions, paragraph 5), Van der Pas, the Director-General, positioned the European Union's views on lifelong learning in the following way:

> Lifelong learning is not a new subject. (...) What is new is the nature of the challenges and the support for action, at the highest political level. On the one hand, European countries are undergoing **a transition towards knowledge-based economies and societies.** Knowledge, competence and the ability to use information intelligently are now important elements – both **to allow individual citizens to participate fully** in society and **to strengthen European competitiveness and economic growth.** (...) On the other hand, there is a broad understanding and support, at the highest political level, that much needs to be done to make lifelong learning a reality for all citizens – not just to promote learning per se but also to help Europe to reach the ambitious objectives set at Lisbon. Although progress has been made (...) **lifelong learning is still far from being a reality for all citizens. 14 million people are still unemployed in Europe.** There are growing **skills gaps** in some sectors of the economy, in particular in the ICT sector. There are also **skills mismatches** right across the board of sectors where people's qualifications and competence, on the one hand, and employers' demands, on the other, do not match. All this hampers the creation of new jobs and **slows down economic growth.** According to one estimate, **the mismatches** between the supply and demand of labour **cost the European Union 100 billion Euro each year.** Therefore, more needs to be done to implement lifelong learning. We need to raise the levels of **investment in human resources.** (...) We need to develop a European strategy for lifelong learning to face the challenges. This is an opportunity that we cannot afford to miss. (Van der Pas, 2001, pp. 11–12; emphasis in original)

The idea that lifelong learning is first and foremost about the development of human capital – an 'investment in human resources' – so as to secure competitiveness and economic growth for Europe clearly echoes a central tenet of an influential document published in 1997 by the OECD, the Organisation for Economic Co-operation and Development, called *Lifelong learning for all* (OECD, 1997). *Lifelong learning for all* also puts a strong emphasis on the economic rationale for lifelong learning understood as learning "throughout life" (OECD, 1997, p. 15). It presents the idea of 'lifelong learning for all' as "the guiding principle for policy strategies that will respond directly to the need to improve the capacity of individuals, families, work-places and communities to continuously adapt and renew" (ibid., p. 13). Adaptation and renewal are considered to be necessary in the face of changes in the global economy and the world of work, including the "large and continuing shift in employment from manufacturing industry to services, the gathering momentum of globalisation, the wide diffusion of information and communications technologies, and the increasing importance of knowledge and skills in production and services" (ibid., p. 13). According to *Lifelong learning for all* the disappearance of many unskilled jobs, the more rapid turnover of products and services, and the fact that people change jobs more often than previously, all point to the need for "more frequent renewal of knowledge and skills" (ibid., p. 13). Lifelong learning "from early childhood education to active learning in retirement" will thus be "an important factor in promoting employment and economic development" (ibid., p. 13). (The sentence continues with "...democracy and social cohesion" – I will return to this below.)

In about three decades, then, the discourse of lifelong learning seems to have shifted from 'learning to be' to 'learning to be productive and employable'. Or, as Peter Jarvis has put it:

> The lifelong learning society has become part of the current economic and political discourse of global capitalism, which positions people as human resources to be developed through lifelong learning, or discarded and retrained if their job is redundant. (Jarvis, 2000, quoted in Grace, 2004, p. 398).

The question this raises is how we should understand these developments and, more importantly, how we should evaluate them.

THE RISE OF THE LEARNING ECONOMY

At one level the trajectory seems to be perfectly clear. Whereas in the past the field of lifelong learning was predominantly informed by a social justice agenda – the 'social purpose' tradition in which adult learning is seen as a lever for empowerment and emancipation (see Fieldhouse, 1996) – the emphasis nowadays is on 'learning for earning' in which adult learning is seen as a lever for economic growth and global competitiveness. As British Prime Minister Tony Blair allegedly has put it: "Education is the best economic policy we have" (Blair, 1998, quoted in Martin, 2002, p. 567). Although at one level this is indeed an adequate depiction of what has happened with lifelong learning in many countries around the world, it is important to look at these developments in more detail so as not to get stuck in unproductive stereotypes. In what follows I wish to make two observations about recent transformations of the field of lifelong learning. I will do this in terms of a simple conceptual model called the 'triangle of lifelong learning,' which I will introduce first.

THE TRIANGLE OF LIFELONG LEARNING

'Lifelong learning' is an elusive concept. It means many things to many people and often means more than one thing at the same time. While the vagueness of the concept makes it possible to connect it to a wide range of different political and ideological agendas, it is important to keep in mind that lifelong learning has probably always carried a number of different meanings, so that any discussion about lifelong learning cannot simply be settled with reference to an alleged original meaning of the idea. In their discussion of the notion of lifelong learning Aspin and Chapman (2001) have made the helpful observation that lifelong learning encompasses a number of different agendas and thus can 'work' for a range of different purposes. Aspin and Chapman make a distinction between three of such purposes which, in their words, are: (1) lifelong learning for *economic progress and development*; (2) lifelong learning for *personal development and fulfilment*; and (3) lifelong learning for *social inclusiveness and democratic understanding and activity* (see Aspin and Chapman, 2001, pp. 39–40).

If we think of lifelong learning as the learning that goes on throughout one's life, that is, the learning that is connected to one's life and the learning that takes place beyond the initial phase of formal education, then there is indeed an aspect of lifelong learning that has to do with the acquisition of new skills and knowledge in relation to the world of work, something that is both important for one's own employability and financial well-being and for the well-being of the economy as a whole. This can be called the *economic function of lifelong learning*. There is also a dimension of lifelong learning that has to do with personal development and fulfil-ment, not only in terms of developing one's potential and talents, but also in terms of learning from the encounters and experiences that make up one's life, finding the 'meaning' of one's life, and maybe even learning to live one's life in a better way (see also Goodson *et al.*, 2010). This is the *personal dimension of lifelong learning*. Thirdly there is a dimension of lifelong learning that has to do with demo-cracy and social justice, with the empowerment and emancipation of individuals so that they become able to live their lives with others in more democratic, just and inclusive ways – which, again, is not only important for the well-being of individuals but for the quality of democratic life itself as well. I will refer to this as the *demo-cratic dimension of lifelong learning*.

While Aspen and Chapman refer to these dimensions as the triangle of lifelong learning, I prefer to depict the interrelationships between these three dimensions in the form of a Venn-diagram of overlapping areas, thus highlighting the fact that life-long learning is more likely to impact on a combination of dimensions rather that that it exists in relation exclusively in relation to one of them. It also means that if we wish to utilise the distinction between the three possible purposes of lifelong learning to characterise developments in policy and practice, it is more likely that we find positions in which more than one function is present, albeit that the relative weight – and also the more precise interpretation – may differ. This becomes visible when we try to characterise the changes that have taken place in the policy and practice of lifelong learning in terms of the distinction between the economic, the personal and the democratic dimension of lifelong learning.

SHIFTING AGENDAS AND SHIFTING CONCEPTIONS OF LIFELONG LEARNING

When we look more closely at the policies and practices of lifelong learning from this angle, it becomes clear that in most cases there is an acknowledgement of the multi-dimensional nature of lifelong learning. This means that differences between positions are more to be understood as differences in emphasis and, more importantly, differences in priorities than that different positions represent only one of the functions of the triangle of lifelong learning.

The authors of the Faure report, for example, are not oblivious to the importance of education for work and economic development. Yet for Faure and his colleagues questions about the economic function of lifelong learning are always subordinate to questions about its democratic function. Whereas the report acknowledges that with respect to "the economy, welfare and standards of living" people in underdeveloped countries "no longer resign themselves so easily to inequality dividing class from class ... as in the days when all was seen as an arrangement by the Almighty," nor that they resign themselves "any more readily to educational underdevelopment, particularly since they have been led to believe that the universalization of education was to become their absolute weapon for the achievement of an economic 'take-off'," the report hastens to add that "the peoples now aspire to democracy *quite independently of their GNP and their rates of school enrolment*" (Faure *et al.*, 1972, p. xxiv, emph. added). Similarly the report acknowledges that although it is the case that motivation for learning largely depends on the search for employment and the desire for learning, the authors do argue that motivation deriving from employment "seems unable to ensure true democratization" (ibid., p. xxix). The Faure-report thus presents us with a vision of lifelong learning in which democratisation is the main driver, and where the basic function of lifelong learning lies in the combination of the personal and the democratic dimension. For Faure the aim of education is 'to enable man to be himself,' yet learning-to-be always has to be understood in democratic terms, that is, as learning-to-be-with-others. This is why the report concludes that uniting '*homo sapiens*' and '*Homo faber*' – the knowing human being and the producing human being – is not enough. What is needed instead is the '*homo concors*,' the human being "in harmony with himself and others" (ibid., p. xxxix).

In the OECD report we can also see an acknowledgement of the composite character of lifelong learning. The mantra throughout the report is that lifelong learning is an important factor in promoting "employment, economic development, democracy and social cohesion" (OECD, 1997, p. 13). The report states, for example, that "a new focus for education and training policies is needed now, to develop capacities to realise the potential of the 'global information economy' and to contribute to employment, culture, democracy and, above all, social cohesion" (ibid., p. 15). In the 'Ministers' Communiqué' attached to the report we can read that the OECD Education Ministers "are all convinced of the crucial importance of learning throughout life for enriching personal lives, fostering economic growth and maintaining social cohesion" (ibid., p. 21) and that "(f)uture economic prosperity, social and political cohesion, and the achievement of genuinely democratic societies with full participation – all depend on a well-educated population" (ibid., p. 24). Even the Director General of the General Directorate for Education and Culture of the European Commission devotes some attention to the theme of 'social inclusion,' arguing that "lifelong learning is not only about employment and adaptability (...) [but] is also a means to personal fulfilment, active citizenship and social inclusion" – although in his view these objectives must be addressed "through policies and processes out-side the employment field" (Van der Pas, 2001, p. 16).

While in all cases, therefore, there is a recognition of the composite nature of life-long learning, the more recent documents present us with a vision of lifelong learning in which economic considerations have become the main driver of lifelong learning and in which the main function of lifelong learning seems to be 'learning for earning,' learning to remain employable and productive in the face of the demands of the new, global economy.

The OECD document is more interesting, not only because it makes mention of the democratic function of lifelong learning, but also because it puts a strong emphasis on the relationships between lifelong learning, social inclusion and "above all, social cohesion." The attention to social inclusion and cohesion could be read as a 'thin' definition of democracy, in which case it might be concluded that the OECD position suffers less from economic reductionism than the view from the European Union does. This would fit rather well with recent interest in the UK into the so-called 'wider benefits of learning' (such as inclusion and cohesion, but also health; see Schuller *et al.*, 2004). While this seems to suggest a turn away from a narrow, economistic approach to lifelong learning, we shouldn't forget, as Schuller (2001, p. 94) has pointed out, that this interest is itself often motivated by assumptions about the importance of such wider benefits for economic performance. And we shouldn't forget that social inclusion is not the same as democracy, particularly not because the discourse of inclusion has the tendency to think of inclusion as including others into one's own definition of inclusion rather than allowing people to set their own terms for inclusion (see Katz, Verducci & Biesta, 2009).

What the triangle of lifelong learning thus helps us to see is how the relationship between the functions of lifelong learning differs in different configurations of life-long learning, and also how this relationship has changed over time. For Faure demo-cracy was the main driver for lifelong learning and although there was a clear emphasis on the personal dimension of lifelong learning as well, personal development and fulfilment is always considered in the light of democratisation, social justice and inter-national solidarity. For Faure *democracy* thus represents an *intrinsic value* whereas personal fulfilment and development occupies a more instrumental position. The eco-nomic dimension is rather separate. For Faure it is not even a necessary condition for the development of democracy. We can see that in more recent approaches the econo-mic function of lifelong learning has taken central position, and we might even say that in the current scheme *economic growth* has become an *intrinsic value*: it is desired for its own sake, not in order to achieve something else. The position of social inclusion and cohesion in this scheme is ambivalent, but it is more likely that they represent instrumental rather than intrinsic values. And we shouldn't forget that social inclusion and cohesion are not necessarily democratic. This brings me to my second observation.

THE INDIVIDUALISATION OF LIFELONG LEARNING AND THE REVERSAL OF RIGHTS AND DUTIES

The other thing that has happened in the field of lifelong learning over the past two decades is the increased *individualisation* of lifelong learning. Perhaps the first thing to note is the way in which this individualisation is expressed in and has in a sense also changed the very language we use to talk about all this. The fact that we nowadays so easily use the phrase 'lifelong learning' already suggests something about the individualisation of the field. Earlier generations, after all, spoke about adult education (see, for example, Lindeman, 1926) or lifelong education (Yeaxlee, 1929) – which is also the phrase used in the Faure-report. Whereas 'education' is a relational concept that, in most cases, refers to the interaction between an educator and a student, 'learning' denotes something that one can do alone and by oneself (see Biesta, 2006). To use a notion like 'the adult learner' or even 'the learner' therefore already indicates a choice for a particular way to configure and conceptualise the field.

The individualisation of lifelong learning is, however, not only a conceptual issue. In his book on the new 'educational order' of lifelong learning Field (2000) has argued, for example, that the actual nature of the learning activities that many adults are engaged in has changed as well. He argues that more and more people are nowadays spending more and more of their time and money on all kinds of different forms of learning, both inside and increasingly also outside and disconnected from the traditional educational institutions. There is not only conclusive evidence that the volume and level of participation in formal adult learning are increasing. There is also a rapidly growing market for non-formal forms of learning, such as in fitness-centres and sport clubs, but also the learning related to self-help therapy manuals, internet learning, self-instructional videos, DVDs, CDs etcetera. One of the most significant characteristics of what Field has called the 'silent explosion of learning' is not only that the new learning is more individualistic – that is, people learning alone and by themselves – but also that the content and purpose of these forms of learning has become more focused on individual issues such as one's body, one's relationships and one's identity. The point is nicely summarised by Boshier. "These days lifelong learning ... denotes the savvy consumer surfing the Internet selecting from a smorgasbord of educational offerings. Learning is an individual activity." (Boshier, 2001, p. 368)

Yet the point is not only that learning has become increasingly an individual *activity*. Under the influence of the learning economy learning has also increasingly become an individual *issue* and an individual *responsibility* (see, for example, Grace, 2004; Fejes, 2004). It is not only that under the imperatives of the learning economy only the economic function of lifelong learning seems to count as 'good' or desirable learning. There is also a clear tendency to shift the responsibility for learning to the individual – or, at a larger scale, to shift this responsibility away from the state towards the private sector. In the learning economy learning ceases to be a collective good and increasingly becomes an individual good. In this scenario the state is less and less a provider and promoter of lifelong learning and increasingly becomes the regulator and auditor of the 'learning market' (see Biesta, 2004[a]).

One way to summarise the individualisation of lifelong learning is to say that it has brought about *a reversal of rights and duties*. Whereas in the past lifelong learning was an individual's right which corresponded to the state's duty to provide resources and opportunities for lifelong learning, it seems that lifelong learning has increasingly become a duty for which individuals need to take responsibility, while it has become the right of the state to demand of all its citizens that they continuously engage in learning so as to keep up with the demands of the global economy. Not to be engaged in some form of 'useful' learning no longer seems to be an option as can, for example, be seen from the recent concern of policy makers with so-called hard-to-reach learners – learners who, for some reason, are not able or not willing to engage in 'learning' and, more specifically, in the kinds of learning demanded by the state and the economy.

WHAT'S THE POINT OF LIFELONG LEARNING?

The individualisation of lifelong learning, and particularly the fact that lifelong learning has become both the individual's responsibility *and* the individual's duty, has several important consequences. The most important one, so I wish to suggest, has to do with the motivation for lifelong learning. The predicament here is that while individuals are being made responsible for their own lifelong learning, the 'agenda' for their learning is mainly set by others. This then raises the question why one should be motivated to learn throughout one's life if decisions about the content, purpose and direction of one's learning are beyond one's own control. What is the point of lifelong learning, so we might ask, if the purpose of lifelong learning cannot be defined by the individual, if, in other words, lifelong learning has no point for the individual who has to 'do' the learning? Should individuals be motivated, for example, by the idea that if they train for the right job this might reduce the current annual loss of 100 billion Euros in the European Union? Should they be motivated by the idea that if they gain the right ICT skills, they will contribute to making Europe the most competitive and dynamic knowledge-based economy in the world?

These are, of course, first and foremost empirical questions which require further investigation. In the context of this chapter I can only suggest that the odd combination of lifelong learning as both the individual's *responsibility* and the individual's *duty* may well have a negative impact on the motivation of adults to engage in lifelong learning. This can at least help us to better understand the particular predicament of individuals in the 'learning economy.' There are three observations that I wish to make in relation to this.

The first point brings us back to the triangle of lifelong learning. If it makes sense to distinguish between the economic, the democratic and the personal function of lifelong learning, then we might also be able to say something about how motivation works differently in each of these areas. The point I wish to make here is that whereas the motivation for the economic function of lifelong learning is predominantly indirect – work is more likely to be valued because of the other things it makes possible, for example through the generation of income, than that it is valued for its own sake (which does not mean, of course, that people cannot gain a sense of satisfaction from their working lives) – the motivation related to the personal and democratic function of lifelong learning is much more direct and intrinsic. If the rise of the learning economy puts the motivation for lifelong learning under pressure we should therefore not forget that the motivation for 'learning for earning' is likely to be already more fragile than the motivation for the personal and democratic dimensions of lifelong learning.

CHAPTER 5

The second thing to keep in mind is that the extent to which individuals will actually experience a contradiction between lifelong learning as a responsibility and lifelong learning as a duty, also depends on their perception and appreciation of the rationale for the development of the learning economy. If adults find the arguments for the learning economy convincing, they may well be very happy to take responsibility for their duty to 'upskill' and retrain throughout their lives. But how strong is this rationale? The official story is that in order to remain competitive in a rapidly changing global economy we need a higher skilled workforce, particularly to serve the knowledge economy, and a more flexible workforce. This, so we are told, is why we need more, better, higher and lifelong education and training, which will eventually bring economic prosperity to nations and individuals. But there are important questions to be asked here. Is it really the case that more and 'better' and higher education leads to economic prosperity? Or is the explanation for the fact that more prosperous economies generally have a better educated workforce to be found in the fact that such economies are able to invest more in education? Is it the case that the workforce as a whole needs higher skills and that we are indeed living in or moving towards a knowledge economy? Or might it be the case that are we experiencing a *polarisation* of work, both within and between societies, where there are pockets of work that require high skills but where the majority of jobs only require a low-skilled, flexible workforce (see, for example, the rise of the call centre industry; Frenkel *et al.*, 1999; Holtgrewe *et al.*, 2002)? There are also more fundamental questions to ask about the wider picture, particularly about the claim that the global economy is simply a fact to which we, as individuals, as nations and as the European Union need to adapt. Could it be the case that economic globalisation is not so much a 'fact' as that it is something that is actively being pursued by some so as to serve the interests of particular nations, groups, classes, companies or individuals? Is economic growth itself a necessity or is it possible to envisage a different future, one based on a different set of values? There is also the question as to whether the learning economy does indeed create prosperity *for all*, or whether it simply reproduces existing economic inequalities, for example between the so-called developed and the so-called developing nations or between the 'haves' and the 'have-nots' within societies. So what's the point of lifelong learning in the learning economy, if at the end of the day lifelong learning continues to benefit *others*?

The third point I wish to make is that the possible contradiction between lifelong learning as an individual's responsibility and a duty may not be a predicament that is only confined to the field of lifelong learning. In his book *Liquid Modernity* (Bauman, 2000) the sociologist Zygmunt Bauman suggests that such contradictions are part of a wider trend in contemporary society. In his book Bauman makes a distinction between two 'phases' of modernity: the old 'solid and heavy' stage of modernity and the contemporary 'liquid and fluid' stage. Bauman argues that modernisation has always implied individualisation, that is, the overcoming of the all-encompassing influence of social, cultural and religious traditions. Individualisation, so he writes, "consists of transforming human 'identity' from a given' into a 'task' and charging the actors with the responsibility for performing that task" (Bauman, 2000, p. 31). Individualisation thus entails the establishment of what Bauman calls *de jure* autonomy (ibid., p. 32). What distinguishes solid from fluid modernity is not the process of individualisation as such, but the 'yawning gap' between the right of self-assertion on the one hand, and the capacity "to control the social settings which render such self-assertion feasible" on the other (ibid., p. 38). For Bauman this is "the main contradiction of fluid modernity" (ibid.), and it is this contradiction, so I wish to suggest, that we can clearly see in the situation of lifelong learners in the learning economy, the situation in which lifelong learners are responsible for their own learning but seem to have little influence on the content, purpose and 'point' of their learning. They have, to use Bauman's words, *de jure* autonomy, but what they seem lacking is *de facto* autonomy. So where do we go from here?

CONCLUSIONS: TOWARDS THE LEARNING DEMOCRACY

In this chapter I have analysed recent transformations in the field of lifelong learning. My focus has been on the consequences of these transformations for individuals and my main claim is that the rise of the learning economy has resulted in a situation where lifelong learning has ceased to be a right and has instead become the individual's duty *and* responsibility. I have suggested that this predicament may well have a negative impact on the individual's motivation for engaging in lifelong learning, particularly the 'learning for earning' that is demanded by the learning economy. I have also suggested that this predicament may not be an exclusive issue for the field of lifelong learning, but may well be characteristic of more general developments in contemporary (post)modern societies.

If we look at these developments from a slight distance, we might say that the lifelong learner is caught up in a struggle over the definition of lifelong learning, a struggle over what counts as 'real' or 'worthwhile' learning. This struggle is not simply conceptual as it impacts directly upon the resources that are made available for lifelong learning. By making lifelong learning a *private* good – something that is considered to be first and foremost valuable in relation to the economic function of lifelong learning and therefore something that is first of all of value to individuals and other players in the economic sector – it becomes increasingly difficult to claim *collective* resources for lifelong learning, particularly resources for supporting the other two dimensions of lifelong learning: the personal and the democratic.

Discussions about the need for the development of a learning economy are often quite dismissive of the personal dimension of lifelong learning. Some proponents of the learning economy have argued that it was about time that adult education 'got real,' and courses in flower arranging and basket weaving are often quoted as examples of the alleged irrelevance of adult education. While proponents of the learning economy may not object to the existence of such learning opportunities as such, they cannot see why collective resources should be made available for the funding of what in their view are strictly private issues. It is here that the interest in the wider benefits of lifelong learning – in this case the wider benefits of *personal* lifelong learning – has a place, since it could be claimed that collective resources should be made available if it were the case that learning for personal fulfilment has a positive impact on such aspects as the individual's health or the development of social capital. While this might positively impact on the availability of resources for the personal function of lifelong learning, it does not mean, of course, that this would imply a recognition of the personal dimension as a collective good. The interest in the wider benefits of lifelong is, after all, first and foremost fuelled by a simple cost-benefit analysis.

What we shouldn't lose sight of in all of this is that lifelong learning is not exhausted by its economic and personal function. The key-question to ask in the light of the recent rise of the learning economy is precisely the question about the relationship between lifelong learning and democracy. Does a democracy need lifelong learning? If so, what kind of lifelong learning does it need? Should we define a democracy as a society that has the capacity and the will to learn about itself? Should we define a democracy as a society that has the ability and the will to learn from the encounter with difference and otherness? Might it be the case that a democracy can only exist as a learning democracy? Should we therefore be worried about the current configuration of lifelong learning in economic terms?

These are not simply rhetorical questions. I believe that we should indeed be concerned about the near-hegemony of the learning economy and that for precisely this reason there is an urgent need to reclaim the democratic dimension of lifelong learning. This is not only in order to bring about a more balanced approach to lifelong learning, one which acknowledges that lifelong learning is a concept with at least three equally important dimensions. The need to reclaim the democratic dimension of lifelong learning also follows from Bauman's observation that the individualisation which is characteristic of fluid modernity – the individualisation that is characterised by a gap between *de jure* autonomy and *de facto* autonomy – signifies a disappearance of the public realm, a disappearance of the realm of democratic politics itself. For Bauman, as we have seen, the main contradiction of fluid modernity lies in the "wide and growing gap between the condition of individuals *de jure* and their chances ... to gain control over their fate and make the choices they truly desire" (Bauman, 2000, p. 39). Bauman argues that this gap "cannot be bridged by individual effort alone" (ibid.). The gap has emerged and grown precisely "because of the emptying of public space, and particularly the 'agora', that intermediary, public/private site ... where private problems are translated into the language of public issues and public solutions are sought, negotiated and agreed for private troubles" (ibid.). This is why Bauman argues that in contemporary individualised society we need "*more, not less, of the 'public sphere'*" (ibid., p. 51; emphasis in original); we need the ability to congeal and condense "private troubles into public interests that are larger than the sum of their individual ingredients ... so that they can acquire once more the shape of the visions of the 'good society' and the 'just society'" (ibid.). What we need, therefore, is more democracy. But democracy is not something that can be produced in the same way as proponents of the learning economy assume that economic growth and competitiveness will follow if people acquire the right skills and qualifications. There is no such thing as a certificate or a diploma in democracy. Democracy, in its shortest formula, is about learning from difference and learning to live with others who are not like us. For this very reason democracy can only be learned *from* life. And this kind of democratic learning is truly a lifelong task.

6

Towards the Learning Democracy

In the previous chapter I have not only indicated how the 'agenda' for lifelong learning has changed over the past decades, but have also asked whether, from the angle of democracy, we should be concerned about the erosion of the democratic rationale for and the democratic dimensions of lifelong learning. This raised a number of questions about the relationships between democracy and lifelong learning, such as whether a democracy needs lifelong learning; if so, what kind of learning it needs; and whether a democracy should perhaps be conceived as a society that has the capacity and will to learn about itself. I summarised this by asking whether it might be the case that a democracy can actually only exist as a learning democracy. In this chapter I engage with these questions is more detail through a discussion of three books that, taken together, provide important insights in the condition of contemporary democratic citizenship and in the (potential) role of learning.

The first book, *Citizenship in Britain: Values, Participation and Democracy* (Pattie *et al.*, 2004) documents the findings from the 'Citizenship Audit,' a large-scale survey conducted in 2000 and 2001 amongst more than 13,000 British adults aged 18 or over. The book provides an overall picture of political participation and voluntary activity in Britain and of the beliefs and values which underpin them and tries to account for the changing nature of British citizenship and the consequences of these changes. Whereas *Citizenship in Britain* gives the macro picture, *Adult Learning, Citizenship and Community Voices* (Coare & Johnston, 2003) very much presents a micro view. Based on a set of case-studies of community-based practices the book tries to unravel and understand the relationships between community-based practice, adult learning, citizenship and democracy. The third title, *Decline of the Public: The Hollowing-out of Citizenship* (Marquand, 2004), introduces a historical and philosophical dimension to the discussion. The book documents the 'rise and fall' of the public domain in British political life and argues that a healthy democracy needs a strong and vibrant public sphere. If a case can be made that adult learning is not something that is private and only of interest to the individual, but belongs to, and to a certain extent even constitutes the public sphere, then we may indeed have reason to be concerned about the impact of the emergence of the learning economy upon the health of democracy in Britain.

CITIZENSHIP IN BRITAIN

As I have shown in chapter 1, many politicians and policy-makers have articulated concerns about the state of democracy in Britain and continue to do so up to the present day. On the one hand they worry about low levels of political participation and understanding; on the other hand they worry about the "seemingly pervasive erosion of the social, political, economic and moral fabric of society" (Kerr, 2000, pp. 74–75). One of the great strengths of Citizenship in Britain is that its authors have made a serious attempt to go beyond the rhetoric in order to provide an empirically-based account of civic life in Britain. Their study, based upon a representative sample of the British population and conducted through a face-to-face survey with 3,528 participants and a mail survey with 9,959 respondents, not only documents the civic attitudes and behaviours of British citizens; it also attempts to provide a explanation of relevant dimensions of citizenship, and tries to give an answer to the 'so what' question by exploring whether communities with strong local civic cultures fare better than communities where civic engagement is weaker.

In the first part of the book the authors provide an overview of civic attitudes and behaviours. With respect to civic attitudes the research suggests that these are generally robust and in a healthy state. People's identification with their country is stronger than with any other territorial formation, they are proud of their British citizenship, they respect the law, do not condone tax evasion, believe that they have a duty to vote, and feel obliged to act in various ways which contribute to the collective good. The British have, however, a selective approach to rights. They believe they have some private rights, such as the right to choose to die, but are less supportive, for example, of homosexuals' rights. With respect to state-provided rights, they are selective as well, in that they are more likely to think that the government has a duty to look after the poor but less likely to believe that the government should provide jobs for the poor. The picture about attitudes towards political institutions reveals that only one in three people is satisfied with British democracy, and the government is regarded as insensitive to majority opinion. People's sense of their political impact is low, although they are more likely to feel that they have influence at local than at national level. Public esteem for politicians is very low and traditional political engagement, such as being a local councillor, attracts little enthusiasm. Nevertheless, people do regard voting as important. The research shows that attitudes vary according to age, gender, occupation, religion, income, education, ethnicity and place, although ethnic background has less importance than the others.

An important conclusion with regard to civic behaviour is that the data appear to show no sign of a public exit from civic engagement. Citizens have not 'contracted out' but are engaged in a multiplicity of political activities. The research does, however, take a broad definition of political activity as encompassing any attempt to influence rules, laws and policies. On this measure three in every four people are engaged in political activity. What is significant is that the most common forms of political activity tend to be the ones that individuals take on their own, like giving money, signing a petition or purchasing particular types of goods, without the need to interact with other people. This is one of the main reasons why the authors say that they could well have called their book 'The Atomised Citizen,' (Pattie *et al.*, 2004, p. 275) since the research clearly shows a rise of individualistic forms of political action. Another key finding is that political engagement is very much dominated by the already well-resourced, that is, the most highly educated, the rich, and those from the top of occupational echelons, which suggests, as the authors rightly emphasise, that political voice must be biased towards those who already possess the greatest resources (see ibid., p. 109). There are similar conclusions about associational life and informal activities, where the research indicates that people are extensively networked. The research reports that two in every three people either belong to an organisation or participate in an informal group or neighbourhood support network, although again the rich, well-educated and those from professional and managerial backgrounds dominate the scene. When looked at the two aspects of associational life separately, the figures are lower. Only one in five of the respondents reports participation in informal networks such as a pub-quiz team, book-reading group, parent-toddler group, or child care group, and only one in three reports to provide active help beyond imme- diate family to ill people, neighbours or acquaintances. Membership of organisations is dominated by 29% who belong to a motoring organisation, with trade union membership in second and sports/outdoor activities in third place (9% and 8% respectively). This shows that organisational membership that matters – rather than simply being an insurance policy against car-breakdown – is much lower. It also highlights the relative importance of sport in the associational life of British citizens (three times more, for example, than membership of religious organisations) (see also Biesta et al., 2001).

In the second part of the book the authors examine the explanatory power of five different theories of citizenship. The authors make a distinction between choice-based theories of citizenship which see citizenship emerging from the choices individual agents make, and structural-based theories of citizenship which see citizenship much more as the outcome of the norms, values and behaviours of the groups to which individuals belong and the society in which they live more generally. Whereas the cognitive engagement theory, one of the two choice-based theories, assumes that participation depends on the individual's access to information and on their ability and willingness to use that information to make informed choices, the general incentives theory focuses much more on the incentives that promote people's participation and engagement. The civic voluntarism model, one of the three structural-based theories, sees civic participation as the outcome of the interaction between resources (time, money and civic skills), civic attitudes such as a sense of political efficacy and in- volvement in politics, and a feeling of obligation to participate (which, itself, is seen as, the product of 'requests for participation' that come from significant others in such social networks as work, family, church, and organisations). The equity-fairness theory focuses the explanation of civic and political participation mainly on the extent to which individuals or groups perceive themselves as disadvantaged in particular situations, which in this theory is considered to be a main motivating factor for becoming politically active. The social capital model provides an explanation of civic participation by focusing on the importance of trust. The willingness to trust strangers is seen as a key factor in the creation of strong social ties which, in turn, is considered to result in high rates of civic engagement and political participation. The authors not only provide a very helpful discussion of the strengths and weak- nesses of each of the theories, but also come up with a very sophisticated examination of the empirical support for each of the theories. Not surprisingly, no single theory dominates the picture, but some models are more important in explaining particular dimensions of citizenship in Britain than others.

With respect to attitudes to rights, for example, the equity-fairness and the civic voluntarism models seem to have the best explanatory power, particularly in understanding that those individuals who feel deprived, who are unemployed, female and members of an ethnic minority are more likely to support state intervention to maintain rights than people in general. A lack of resources, in other words, appears to generate a demand for rights. The general incentives theory and the social capital model, on the other hand, are more important in understanding the factors that influence the 'obligation to volunteer' dimension of citizenship, which includes positive attitudes towards voluntary action and civic service and obedience to the law. The general incentives model plays an important role in understanding individualistic political participation (such as donating money, signing a petition, buying goods for political or ethical reasons), whilst collective political action is better explained by the cognitive engagement model, in that respondents who are interested in politics and who are educated beyond secondary school are more likely to participate in collective action. An important finding is that social capital only seems to have a weak influence on participation and volunteering if it is defined in terms of membership of formal and informal groups, and that no support can be found for the idea that trust promotes such participation. The influence of the trust variable is either absent or appears to have a negative rather than a positive impact.

In the third and final part of the book the authors explore relationships between local differences in the quality of citizenship and the quality of life, defined in terms of outputs (the level of public services) and outcomes (the perceived quality of public services). Whereas the quality of citizenship does not seem to influence the level of outputs, it does have an impact on outcomes – which makes the authors conclude that good citizenship does have a generally positive bearing on the quality of life. What is interesting in this account, as least from a theoretical point of view, is that their explanation of the relationship between citizenship and outputs and outcomes again generates some conclusions that are in contradiction with the expectations from social capital theory. In those cases the 'suburban democracy' thesis based on research by Oliver (1999; 2000) – an approach which suggests that political activity will be higher in heterogeneous than in homogeneous communities – seems to provide a better explanatory framework. The authors also try to say something about the dynamics of citizenship by comparing findings from the 2000 and 2001 wave of their data-collection. While the data do suggest an increase in civic attitudes and behaviours, which leads the authors to the conclusion that Britain was a more civic society after the 2001 election than it had been before it, the empirical basis for this conclusion seems not to be very robust.

In the final chapter the authors draw some important conclusions. They begin by reiterating their main finding: citizens in Britain have not contracted out of political participation, but the nature of their participation has become more individualistic. While there are many 'good citizens – those who are aware of their rights and obligations and who participate actively in voluntary and political activities – there are also 'bad' citizens: those who want rights without acknowledging their obligations.

The authors hasten to add, however – and this is a very important point – that this primarily concerns individuals who lack power and resources. Yet these individuals are at the very same time those who are least likely to participate in political activity. This leads to the worrying observation that Britain is (still) divided between "a well-connected group of citizens with prosperous lives and high levels of civic engagement and other groups whose networks, associational life and involvement in politics is very limited" (Pattie *et al.*, 2004, pp. 267–268).

The individualisation of citizenship not only concerns the modes of participation, but is also manifest in the fact that organisations in the public sphere have become increasingly defined around more individualistic issues, something which is evident in the rise of interest and advocacy groups. What is happening here can be characterised as the erosion of solidarity or, as the authors put it, as the emergence of a situation in which "no one has an incentive to accept costs whereas everyone has an incentive to seek benefits" (ibid., p. 276). This development is closely connected to the emergence of a new type of citizen identity, that of the citizen as a consumer of public services. As I have argued elsewhere in more detail (see Biesta, 2006, chapter 1), the rise of the citizen-as-consumer goes hand in hand with the rise of the government as a provider, and entails a transformation of the relationship between the state and its citizens from a political into an economic relationship. What is at stake in this transformation, as the authors of Citizenship in Britain make clear, is "a decline in the dialogue between the rulers and the ruled – a decline in deliberation" (ibid., p. 278), which can be taken as a sign of the decline of democracy itself (see below). It is for these reasons that the potential implications of the rise of the atomised citizen may be more worrying than the authors seem to believe. The key question here, to put it briefly, is whether the atomised citizen can actually still be called a citizen, or whether atomised citizenship is an oxymoron.

Can the tide be turned? The authors are very aware that many of the factors that contribute to 'good' citizenship are difficult to control and seem to be at odds with the direction in which British society is developing. The four suggestions they make for the strengthening of citizenship – citizenship education in schools, devolution of power to the locality and regions, a reduction of political 'spin,' and the creation of an inclusive and equal society with strong common norms and values – do make sense, although, as the book itself shows, some of the problems around British citizenship run deeper and may not necessarily be addressed by acting upon these suggestions. By showing that 'bad' citizenship is more often the effect of a lack of resources rather than the outcome of the 'wrong' values and attitudes, the book also provides a compelling argument against the idea that individuals are to blame for an alleged crisis in democracy and that 'lessons in citizenship' – for the young and the old – will suffice to address the crisis. It also shows the crucial importance of people's actual condition of citizenship for their perceptions and motivations.

There is, however, a remarkable omission in Citizenship in Britain in that the book says hardly anything at all about the role of (adult) learning in understanding citizenship. While the research does document the level of formal education of the participants, this factor is only used as an independent variable in the explanation of differences in citizenship attitudes and behaviours (and in all cases it turns out to be a significant factor). What the research does not make visible, however, is what people learn as a result of their actual 'condition of citizenship' – which includes the resources available to them and the extent to which they feel that they can influence the conditions that shape their lives – nor how such learning, in turn, impacts upon their citizenship attitudes and behaviours. Do people who have positive experiences with democratic action become better democrats and more committed citizens? And are those who are disenfranchised, either because of a lack of resources or because of a lack of positive experiences with democratic action, on a trajectory that makes them less and less interested in democratic citizenship? Participation in adult education is also remarkably absent from the list of organisational memberships, nor does it figure in the examples of informal associational life. We might speculate that the latter partly reflects the transformations in the field of adult learning mentioned in the previous chapter, although it seems more likely that it never occurred to the authors to ask questions about this aspect in the first place (education is not listed in the survey questions about formal and informal associational activity). We also shouldn't forget, of course, that the Citizenship Audit is primarily a cross-sectional study, whilst questions about the influence of learning on citizenship can only be properly addressed with a longitudinal design. And we shouldn't forget that whilst survey research is powerful in discerning patterns between a large set of variables, we need another type of research in order to understand the underlying processes. This is precisely what the next book offers.

ADULT LEARNING AND THE PRACTICE OF CITIZENSHIP

Adult Learning, Citizenship and Community Voices (Coare & Johnston, 2003) brings together the insights and experiences of academic researchers and practitioners around the complex relationships between learning and citizenship, viewed through the lens of community-based action. The first part of the book sets out the general framework for the book and provides information about the social and historical context of the discussion about adult learning and citizenship. In the first chapter Johnston documents the economic, political, social and cultural changes that characterise contemporary society. Globalisation, pluralisation and individualisation have led to a situation in which citizens need to learn anew "how to understand their own situation, how to fit into society and how to question it and how to exercise their rights and responsibilities as citizens, both individually and collectively" (ibid., p. 7). Johnston complements this with an overview of different traditions in adult education and their approaches to citizenship. Whereas the liberal tradition focuses on the enlightenment of the individual whilst underestimating the role of wider socio-economic conditions and constraints, the radical tradition has a tendency to focus too much on the public and political dimensions of citizenship whilst ignoring private and personal aspects. Johnston presents the community approach to adult education as a way to overcome the one-sidedness of the other two approaches. The community approach offers the prospect of a "grounded particularity which takes (local) account of both structure and agency, recognises different identities and cultures and makes a situated link between the private and the public" (ibid., p. 16).

Thus a community adult education approach, so Johnston suggests, "can look towards a reconciliation of the critical structural analysis of the radicals and a more specific social purpose of liberal adult education" (ibid., p. 16).

Johnston is aware that these claims need to be examined critically – and the purpose of this edited collection is precisely to do so through the presentation of a series of cases studies within a wider framework of citizenship, learning and community-based practice. Johnston does notice some of the dangers of the community-based approach to adult education, amongst them most notably the danger of a 'romantic localism' which forgets that the community contexts is part of wider socio-political processes. He is well aware that in advanced capitalist countries "a community orientation has too often meant no more than a localised marketing and consumerist focus on a predictable and largely reproductive curriculum" (ibid., p. 18). But this need not necessarily be the case. At its best community education "can offer a space for learning that is somewhat removed from more formal educational provision and therefore a learning context which is not unduly influenced or shaped by institutional norms or requirements" which allows scope "for a range of different learning engagements" and "for the development of 'voice' that is such an integral part of participation and active citizenship" (ibid., p. 18). Along these lines, Johnston suggests, community-based adult education may even have the potential of a "reinvention of politics as local level" (ibid.).

This potential is closely related to one of the four (overlapping) dimensions of adult learning that are part of a framework Johnston presents for understanding the relationships between learning and citizenship, namely adult learning for active citizenship (the other three dimensions are: adult learning for inclusive citizenship, for pluralistic citizenship and for reflexive citizenship). Adult learning for active citizenship focuses on "the crucial link between learning and action" and involves learning by doing "across a wide spectrum of civil society" (ibid., p. 62). Johnston suggests that there might be a 'hard-soft continuum' of learning contexts, "ranging from local learning groups, to study-circles, to voluntary organisations, to different types of community groups to social and popular movements" (ibid.). Common to all these groups is that they are involved in learning and that they "are trying to promote and develop their individual and collective 'voice'" (ibid.). In the context of a discussion of the potential of these different types of groups, Johnston refers to a growing body of research evidence which indeed shows that involvement in the activities of these groups leads to learning that has a positive impact on citizenship (see, for example, Merrifield, 1997; Elsdon, 1997; Larsson, 2001). The role for the adult educator in these processes, Johnston argues, has to be a modest one. In order to avoid dangers of either 'colonisation' or 'tokenistic engagement,' any initiative should try to be as much as possible "on the terms and on the territory of individuals, social groups or movements and outside the immediate imperialist gaze of educational institutions" (ibid., p. 64).

Coare adds some important observations about citizenship in her introductory chapter to the volume. In a brief historical overview of citizenship in Britain, she points to the Thatcher government as the one that didn't simply reform the civic contract between the state and citizens, but rather 'ripped it up' (see ibid., p. 43).

With Thatcher, citizenship became a question of moral rather than political virtue, and individuals were made responsible for their own social and economic well-being. Coare rightly observes, however, that to assert one's rights as a citizen and to do one's citizenship duty, one needs resources: "knowledge, networks, time and an identifiable 'voice'" (ibid., p. 45), which is precisely why the idea of making individuals responsible for their citizenship without paying attention to the resources that define their condition of citizenship, is problematic. Coare also mentions the impact of the 'economic imperative' on lifelong learning opportunities. The point here is that although there has been a clear extension of lifelong learning opportunities for adults on the basis of an inclusion agenda, the aim of such policies has primarily been to enable adults "to participate more fully in the economic life of the community and country, rather than in its political life" (ibid., p. 46). Taken together, these observations prompt her to make a case for "creating the conditions and opportunities that enable people to act as citizens" (ibid., p. 48).

With their introductory chapters the editors take a clear position in the discussion about the role and function of adult learning in contemporary society. They suggest that community-based practice may have a lot to offer in providing a space for citizenship learning and citizenship action. Do the seven case studies that form the second part of the book live up to these expectations? Not surprisingly, some of them do, some don't. The chapter by Bellis and Morrice focuses on the experiences of refugees and asylum seekers in establishing themselves as citizens in British society. The small project on which the chapter is based highlights the importance of educational provision, such as learning English and understanding the complexities of British society, but also makes visible that most of the provision and the underlying policy is based upon a deficit model, one that assumes that all refugees and asylum seekers have a similar lack that needs to be filled with the same package of language, IT and citizenship lessons. It is not inconceivable that this produces an experience of second class citizenship, which may well function as a 'lesson' in citizenship with much stronger impact on the citizenship attitudes and behaviours of refugees and asylum seekers than the official classes in British citizenship. Whilst the participants in the project all emphasise the importance of inclusion and a sense of belonging to British society, the authors emphasise that "inclusion should not mean assimilation (...) but a recognition of existing skills, talents and knowledge and a celebration of distinctive cultural diversity and fluidity" (ibid., p. 89).

While the experience of refugees and asylum seekers connects citizenship and learning by focusing on the implicit learning as a result of the condition of citizenship of people in these groups, the chapter by Moore on the learning involved in ecological activism, provides a more familiar picture of how involvement in political activism can be an important and empowering learning experience for participants. The important dimension added by the chapter on non-violent civil disobedience in protests against logging of rainforests in Canada, is that it questions the universal validity of the idea of the 'good' citizen as the 'obedient' citizen. The example of ecological activism shows that the 'good' citizens are actually the ones who stand up against the government, who resist policies on the basis of a set of (ecological) values that differs clearly from the values that inform government action (in this case predominantly economic values). Rather than learning for social inclusion, the chapter shows the importance of adult learning that leads to (justified) social exclusion – and presents this as an important dimension of a different conception of 'good' citizenship. Another interesting aspect is that the protests are not only presented as a learning experience for the participants; through their activism the participants also aim to educate the wider public. As a Welcome Handout given to participants at the peace camp puts it: "We are here to bear witness to the destruction, to peacefully resist that destruction, and to educate ourselves and the public about these issues." (ibid., p. 103; emphasis added).

In contrast to the self-directed learning of ecological activist, the chapter by Cairns on citizenship learning in relation to regeneration policies and practices in the UK, provides a perceptive analysis of the learning opportunities that are part of a community regeneration project. While it can be argued that the UK Neighbourhood Renewal strategy should be welcomed because, unlike many of the 'moral' and educational attempts to address the crisis in democracy in Britain, this strategy actually aims to improve the material conditions of many citizens, the chapter shows that there is a real danger that the agenda of the local communities and voluntary groups that should be at the heart of the process, become colonised by professionals and the 'deliverers' of neighbourhood renewal. Rhona, one of the participants in the New Deal for Communities (NDC) programme, gives a very astute account of the problem.

When I read the [NDC] leaflet it was brilliant! It said the NDC would empower local people [...] to be able to run whatever projects have been set up, to give them the experience and the expertise so they can get an education so their lives would be better. So they're saying we residents actually have some power and are to be consulted? No! Because management make the decisions. (ibid., p. 114)

What these, and other case studies in the book reveal, is first of all that forms of civic action and participation in associational life do indeed provide important experiences and opportunities for citizenship learning for those who take part. This is not to suggest that all experiences are positive and that all learning has a positive impact on citizenship attitudes and behaviours. The case studies provide examples both of positive and negative experiences, and both of positive and negative impact on further citizenship action. What also transpires from several of the case studies is the crucial importance of the actual condition of people's citizenship. If the predominant experience is one of exclusion or lack of power, citizens often draw negative conclusions. Dorney's and Hodgon's account of the experiences of 'excluded' young people reveals the many "anti-citizenship lessons" (p. 144) that these young people picked up in the realities of their daily lives, particularly the "numerous incidences of abuse of state and institutional power to which they had either been victim or witness" (ibid.). Their chapter also documents, however, that the creation of a space which provides basic emotional and practical support *first*, can become a space for citizenship learning and even, as the authors argue, "a physical citizenship space" (ibid., p. 149).

In the third and final part of the book, the editors come to similar conclusions. Of particular value are their reflections on the possible role of the adult educator.

They argue for adult educators to work *with* communities rather than *on* them and argue for the adoption of a 'liberating' educational approach "which first acknowledges the structural inequalities that impact on people's lives, then use these as critical starting points from which to help learner/citizens explore and develop any subsequent learning, agency or active citizenship" (ibid., p. 206). More practically, they present ten propositions about what adult educators can do in supporting and promoting citizenship in a range of different learning contexts. These include: promoting social learning, building social capital, fostering collective identities, finding common purpose, listening to voices, negotiating the curriculum, connecting informal and formal learning, embracing participation, working with social movements and influencing policy (see ibid., pp. 207–219). In all this they envisage the adult educator to be more than simply a facilitator. Adult educators have more to offer than simple 'process management' skills. Although the 'technical agency' of the adult educator is important, particularly to acknowledge that the people adult educators are working with are already learning and in order to respect the autonomy of learners, there can be an additional need for the 'political agency' of adult educators, particularly with those "who are not in a position to identify their needs" (ibid., p. 220; see also Biesta, 2006, chapter 1). An important dimension of the political agency of adult educators, so I wish to suggest, has to do with their role in the 'translation' of the needs and interests of particular groups into *common* or *public* concerns. The role of the adult educator is not simply to make the needs and wants of a particular group visible, but to place their needs and wants in a wider context so that they can begin to see that their struggles are connected with the struggles of others with different, and sometimes even conflicting needs and wants. As Coare and Johnson put it, quoting Thompson: "community education can build bridges between people in divided communities" and "help to repair damaged solidarities" so as to contribute "to an engaged and reflexive solidarity among different groups in a range of community contexts" (ibid., p. 211). This not only suggests that adult educators need to operate in the public rather than the private sphere. It also suggests that citizenship learning itself has to take place in the public sphere – otherwise, to reiterate a point made above, there is no good reason for calling it *citizenship* learning.

THE DECLINE OF THE PUBLIC?

David Marquand's *Decline of the public* (Marquand, 2004) has as its subtitle *the hollowing-out of citizenship*. Marquand doesn't use a question mark in the title of his book. For him it is perfectly clear that the public domain is in crisis, that this crisis is the result of twenty years in which 'an aggressively interventionist state' has systematically enfeebled the institutions and practices that nurtured the public domain, and that this has hollowed out the possibilities for citizenship. Since the public domain is a 'gift of history,' not of nature, a reinvention of the public domain is not impossible. However, such a reinvention cannot simply be a return to the public domain of old days. Before we try to reinvent a notion of the public domain, so Marquand argues, we need to understand the history of its emergence and the history of its recent decline – which is precisely what Marquand tries to do in the four chapters preceding his 'counter-attack' (ibid., p. 116).

Marquand characterises the public domain as a *dimension* of social life, not as a sector of it. It is a dimension with its own norms and decision rules, a 'set of activities' which can be carried out by private individuals, private charities and even private firms as well as public agencies. It is 'symbiotically linked' to the notion of a public interest, in principle distinct from private interests, and central to it are the values of citizenship, equity and service. In it goods are distributed on the basis of need and not of personal ties or access to economic resources. The public domain is not only *different* from the private domain "of love, friendship and personal connection" and from the market domain "of buying and selling", of "interest and incentive," (p. 4); it is also *separate* from both these domains. The public domain is "a space, protected from the adjacent market and private domains, where strangers encounter each other as equal partners in the common life of the society" (ibid., p. 27). The key-function of the public domain is to define the public interest and to produce public goods (see p. 26). It is the domain where citizens collectively define what the public interest is to be, "through struggle, argument, debate and negotiation" (p. 33). This implies that the values "that sustain, and are in turn sustained by, the public domain" (p. 57) are not the values of self-interest but of *collective* interest. Given that collective interest may sometimes go against one's immediate self-interest, engagement with and commitment to the public domain – another name for citizenship – implies "a certain discipline" and "a certain self-restraint" (ibid., p. 57). Marquand emphasises that this does not come naturally but has to be "learned and then internalized, sometimes painfully," which is why he argues that the implementation of these values in a real-world society requires nothing less than "a cultural and ideological revolution" (ibid.).

Marquand convincingly shows that this revolution was essentially "a Victorian achievement – albeit one that the twentieth century built on extensively" (ibid., p. 41). "The great work of the Victorian era was to carve out from the encircling market and private domains a distinct, self-conscious and vigorous public domain governed by non-market and non-private norms, and to erect barriers protecting it from incursions by its market and private neighbours." (ibid.) Given the way in which the public domain was won from the private and the market domain, it is not surprising that its erosion over the past decades is precisely the outcome of incursions from both the private and the market domain. Marquand has many important things to say about the "revenge of the private" (ibid., p. 79), the protest against the "hard, demanding, 'unnatural' austerities of public duty and public engagement in the name of authenticity and sincerity" (ibid.) and particularly shows how identity politics, understood as the idea that "the private self should be omni-competent and omni-present" (ibid., p. 80) has made deliberative politics of any sort "virtually impossible" (ibid., p. 82). The main focus of the book, however, is on the ways in which the logic of the market domain, both directly and through the way in which this logic has been adopted by Conservative governments since the mid-seventies, has colonised and eroded the public domain. For Marquand this is not simply a process in which the market has intruded the public and private sphere; it is a process in which the neo-liberal values of self-interest and utility maximisation have become the core values of British government in the last quarter of the 20th century – which is why he sees the process first and foremost as a '*Kulturkampf*', a clash of political cultures and political values.

Although the neo-liberal combination of 'market mimicry' and 'central control' (ibid., p. 114) is first and foremost the hallmark of Thatcherism, and although Marquand emphasises that "Blair is not Thatcher in drag" (ibid., p. 116), he does make the case that for the most part "Blair and his colleagues have followed the previous regime's approach to the public domain" (ibid., p. 117; see also Biesta, 2010[a], chapter 3). 'New Labour' has pushed marketisation and privatisation forward; it displayed a fundamental distrust in professionals; its rhetoric was saturated with the language of consumerism; and though it sometimes spoke the language of community, it refused to acknowledge "that community loyalties can be forged only in a social realm protected from market power" (ibid., p. 118). Marquand does acknowledge that to a certain extent the public domain has survived – and the examples he gives largely coincide with the evidence about civic participation from the Citizenship Audit. Yet for Marquand these are mainly "blips on a downward curve" (ibid.), partly because the public-interest argument no longer seems to play a role in contemporary politics – debates about the future of public services, for example, are quintessentially about the private interests of individual consumers – and partly because there is no longer a place nor a space for public deliberation and contestation about the common good.

Marquand paints a rather bleak picture of the state of democracy in Britain at the dawn of the 21st century. But a lot of what he has to say not only rings true but is actually supported by the findings from the Citizenship Audit. The atomised citizen, for example, might well be seen as the citizen that has lost its 'natural habitat,' that is, the public domain. Marquand adds historical detail and philosophical analysis to the findings from the Citizenship Audit. Although he does so from a perspective that is clearly normative in that it is informed by a public domain ethos, it is this perspective which allows him to reveal the democratic deficit of British politics and political life. One important conclusion from his analysis is that we shouldn't understand public disenchantment, the 'retreat from citizenship,' as a *cause* of the hollowing out of citizenship, but rather as a *response* to this hollowing out, a response to the fact that there are less and less opportunities for citizens to *be* citizens, to have a say in the contestation and deliberation about the common good. New Labour might have said that it wanted to give the citizens of Britain more choice. But, as I have argued elsewhere (Biesta, 2010[a]), democracy is not about choice. Or to be more precise: democracy is not about choice from a set-menu but is concerned with choosing which options should be on the menu in the first place.

Marquand's suggestions for the reinvention of the public domain take the form of a list of thirteen propositions for a public philosophy that might inform such a reinvention. The propositions are mainly based on his analysis of the intrusion from the side of the market – which is why he argues for a belief in the possibility of public interest, an emphasis on trust, a need to protect the public domain from incursion by the market and private domains, a clear distinction between the market identity of the consumer and the political identity of the citizen, professional autonomy, and a political system that puts checks and balances on state power. (Surprisingly, his propositions do not deal with countering the effects of the erosion of the public domain from the side of the private sphere.)

What is most significant in the context of this essay is the role learning plays in Marquand's argument. On the one hand, as we have seen, Marquand argues that the public domain ethos does not come naturally – which also means that it does not come easily – but that it has to be learned, and the best way to learn it is through participation in the public domain. But learning not only figures in Marquand's explanation of how the public domain ethos is formed. Learning is also central in Marquand's view of a reinvented public domain. He argues that if the public domain is to be re-invented, the government needs to learn a new approach to governance – "an approach based on the notion of social learning, in which 'key participants in the policy process ... come together for discussion and debate'" (ibid., p. 140). This implies that the state "ceases to be a commander or a controller, and becomes a learner along with other learners" (ibid.). Such processes of social learning need diversity, pluralism and difference because, as he puts it, "it would be hard ... to learn anything, in a class consisting of the teacher's clones" (ibid., p. 141). Differences, however, need protection and this is why Marquand believes that we need "self-confident and powerful Intermediate institutions" such as "local and regional authorities, universities, trade unions, professions, NGOs, the judiciary and the rest" – not just "to protect the public domain from market and private power, but also to protect it from an inherently over-intrusive state" (ibid.).

CONCLUSIONS

With these remarks we have come full circle. One thing that might be concluded from the books discussed in this chapter is that there is indeed a crisis in democracy. But what the books help us to see is that this crisis is not located where many politicians think it is located. With Marquand I am inclined to believe that it is not the lack of people's civic and political engagement that has led to a crisis in democracy. It rather is the crisis in everyday democracy, manifested in the limited opportunities for democratic experience and democratic practice in the actual lives of many people that has brought about civic and political disengagement. If this is true, then it means that an effective response to the crisis in democracy should not focus on more education, on more lessons in 'good'; citizenship, but should instead focus on the actual condition of people's citizenship. The only way to combat a lack of democracy, to put it differently is with more democracy. What many of the case studies in *Adult learning, citizenship and community voices* show, is the crucial role of learning – particularly collective, action-based learning – in actual practices and processes of democratisation. The case studies show how adult learning can make community action into a reflexive process, one which, amongst other things, helps participants to see beyond their immediate interests and to understand that their empowerment has to be connected with the empowerment of others. Along these lines the cases studies provides examples of the kind of learning democracy that

Marquand envisages. This, in turn, shows that adult learning cannot be understood as something private that is only of interest to the individual. Adult learning has a crucial role to play in a democracy, and a case might even be made that a democracy can indeed only exist as a learning democracy, which is precisely why we should be concerned about the recent 'economisation' and 'individualisation' of the field of adult learning. The second book in this review provides glimpses of what a learning democracy might look like. The first book makes clear *that* we need it, whilst the third book provides a strong argument *why* we need it – now even more than ever.

7

Theorising Civic Learning: Socialisation, Subjectification and the Ignorant Citizen

In the previous chapters I have made a case for shifting the focus from the teaching of citizenship to the multifarious ways in which democracy is learned in schools, colleges and universities, and in society at large. I have argued that the processes and practices that make up the everyday lives of children, young people and adults – as they are lived both within and outside of a range of different institutions – convey important and often influential 'lessons' in democratic citizenship. Some of these lessons are positive, but quite often the messages are mixed or even negative, both with regard to the value of democratic processes and practices and with regard to the ways in which individuals are positioned as citizens and are able (or not) to enact their citizenship. What children, young people and adults learn from these experiences is therefore strongly influenced by what I have referred to as their actual condition of citizenship. This immediately shows that if policy makers and politicians wish to improve the attitudes and behaviours of citizens, they would be well advised to invest in the actual conditions of people's citizenship. This encompasses both the basic material conditions of people's lives and the wider material, social and symbolic resources needed for democratic participation and action. In this respect I agree wholeheartedly with Marquand's observation that any retreat from citizenship or any wider 'crisis' in democracy should not be seen as the cause of the hollowing out of citizenship, but rather as a response to this hollowing out, a response, that is, to the reduction of opportunities for democratic engagement, contestation, deliberation and participation and opportunities for translating private troubles into collective issues.

From this angle many of the developments I have reviewed in the preceding chapters – such as the place of citizenship in the Scottish Curriculum for Excellence and in European Higher Education policy, the developments in understanding the civic role of the University, and the transformations in the field of adult education and lifelong learning – all seem to go in the opposite direction. They all display a strong tendency to focus the discussion on individuals and their responsibilities and duties, to highlight the social more than the political dimensions of citizenship, and to see democracy more in terms of consensus and sameness than in terms of contestation and difference. The convergence in policy thinking and policy rhetoric is both remarkable and worrying. It is remarkable for the very fact that discussions in a fairly wide range of different domains and geographical locations all seem to follow a similar pattern. This, in itself, does not have to be a reason for concern if, that is, it could be shown that the choices made are the outcome of a careful consideration of available options. Yet the developments I have discussed in previous chapters do not give the impression that this has actually been the case. This gives extra weight to some of the criticisms I have presented, not in the least Westheimer's and Kahne's rather devastating conclusion that a responsible citizen does not necessarily have to be a democratic citizen.

The developments discussed in the preceding chapters also entail views about education and learning. One trend that can be discerned is that there is often more attention to the purposes of citizenship education, that is, to views about what kind of citizens children and young people should become, than that there is about the processes and practices that should bring this about. One question this raises is how we should understand the learning processes that are involved, and it is to this question – the question of what I will refer to as civic learning – that I will turn in this chapter.

CIVIC LEARNING

If, as I have suggested, civic learning is the learning which occurs in and through the processes and practices that make up the everyday lives of children, young people and adults and which is closely connected to their actual condition of citizenship, then, unlike what is assumed in much curricular thinking, we should not conceive of civic learning as a linear process moving from a situation of not-yet-being-a-citizen to a situation of fully-fledged citizenship. Civic learning should rather be understood as *non-linear*, and also as *recursive*, and *cumulative*. Civic learning is a *non-linear* process because it is closely connected to ongoing positive and negative experiences with democracy and citizenship, and thus is likely to reflect fluctuations in these experiences. Also civic learning is not simply the result of everyday experiences with democracy and citizenship but also feeds back into these experiences, which is the reason for calling civic learning a *recursive* process. Although civic learning is not a linear process, it is important to see that it is *cumulative* because positive and negative experiences in the past cannot simply be eradicated and will influence future action and learning.

Whereas the fact that civic learning non-linear, recursive and cumulative points at the formal characteristics of civic learning – that is, characteristics that follow from the definition of civic learning as the learning connected to everyday experiences and practices – there is one further more substantive distinction that, in my view, is crucial for the discussion about civic learning and citizenship education. This is the distinction between forms of civic learning that contribute to the reproduction of the existing socio-political order and thus to the adaptation to or insertion of individuals into this order, and those forms of civic learning that contribute to political subjectivity and agency. As I have already briefly mentioned in chapter 3, I propose to refer to these two different forms of civic learning as a *socialisation* conception of civic learning and a *subjectification* conception (for these terms see also Biesta, 2010[a], chapter 1). In terms of the aims of civic learning and citizenship education, the first would see the aims of civic learning first and foremost in terms of the reproduction of an existing socio-political order and thus of the adaptation of individuals to this order, while the second would focus on the emergence of political agency and thus sees the aims of civic learning first and foremost in terms of the promotion of political subjectivity and agency.

The strong focus on individuals and on their knowledge, skills and dispositions, the emphasis on a community of sameness rather than a community of difference, and the wider functionalism that can be found in views about citizenship and citizenship education discussed in the previous chapters, reveal a strong tendency to conceive of civic learning predominantly in terms of socialisation. This raises an important more theoretical question, because if it is the case that the 'essence' of democracy can indeed be expressed as a particular, well-defined singular order, then citizenship can be understood as a positive identity – that is, an identity that can be fully expressed and defined – and thus civic learning can be fully understood in terms of the acquisition of this identity by individuals. In that case a socialisation conception of civic learning would not only be justified; one could even say that this would be the *only* way to understand civic learning. If it could be argued, however, that there is more to democracy than this; if it could be argued, in other words, that democracy always escapes its own full determination, than there could be a need for a different conception of civic learning and also for different processes and practices of civic learning than those captured in the idea of socialisation.

It is this question which I will entertain in the remainder of this chapter in order to build a case for the need to distinguish between a socialisation and a subjectification conception of civic learning. I will develop my argument by looking at four dimensions of democracy and democratic politics: the nature and character of democratic communities, the borders of such communities, the processes that occur within such communities and the status of those who engage in such processes. In relation to each dimension I will present views that focus on order and views that raise questions about the extent to which democracy and democratic politics can and should be understood in terms of order. For my discussion I draw inspiration from the work of Chantal Mouffe and Jacques Rancière, who both have raised important questions about the limitations of an 'ordered' understanding of democratic politics. With Mouffe and Rancière I argue for a conception of democratic politics which, in some respect, is 'beyond' order. It is on the basis of such a more 'anarchical' view of democracy and democratic politics that I make my case for the importance of a subjectification conception of civic learning as distinct from a socialisation conception.

THE POLITICAL COMMUNITY: 'ARCHIC' OR ANARCHIC?

In her book *Political Theory and the Displacement of Politics* (Honig, 1993), Bonnie Honig raises the question whether democratic politics depends on the existence of a well-defined community within which democracy can take place, or whether it is the very establishment of such communities that is the most important 'moment' in democratic politics. Honig supports the latter view, arguing that when democratic politics is restricted to those who already agree on the basic rules of the political game, the most important and most difficult aspect of democratic politics, that is, the process though which such an agreement about basic rules is achieved, is left out of the picture. This not only means that it is left out of our *understanding* of the dynamics of democratic politics, but also that it runs the risk of being beyond the *reach* of democratic contestation. This is why she maintains that those political theories and philosophies in which it is argued that politics is only for those who are like-minded – those who subscribe to a basic set of rules and values – actually contribute to a *displacement* of politics rather than that they are able to capture the 'essence' of democratic politics.

Honig published her book during the heydays of discussions between liberalism and communitarianism. The importance of Honig's intervention in this particular debate lay in her observation that with regard to their views about the nature of the political community, liberals and communitarians actually deploy a similar way of thinking where the act of the construction of the political community is itself seen as something that *precedes* politics proper. While communitarians openly enact the displacement of politics when they argue that politics is only possible on the basis of a shared set of values and principles, Honig shows – particularly through a discussion of the early work of John Rawls – that liberalism operates according to a similar template when it articulates 'entry conditions' for participation in democratic politics. In the early work of Rawls, that is the work before his *Political Liberalism* (1996), these entry conditions – a minimum level of rationality and a minimum level of morality – were considered to be natural and non- or pre-political rather than that they were seen as articulating particular *political* values. (In later work Rawls came to acknowledge much more explicitly the political underpinnings of liberalism.)

One of the important contributions made by Chantal Mouffe in this discussion is not only that she has exposed the political nature of such entry conditions by emphasising that such conditions always do political 'work' in including some and excluding others (see, for example, Mouffe, 1993). She has also argued that we should be explicit about these exclusions because it is only then that we can begin to understand that those who are excluded from the political community are not 'outside' because of a lack of rationality of morality – also because what counts as rational and moral is at least partly the 'effect' of the particular hegemonic construction of 'inside' and 'outside' – but because their political values are different from those who are on the inside (see also below). Whereas Mouffe would disagree with (some forms of) liberalism and to a lesser extent with communitarianism about how we should understand the political community, she agrees with both liberals and communitarians that the practice of democratic politics requires stability and order, albeit that the construction of this order is always a political act and, more importantly, an act that is always up for contestation and revision. But because democratic politics cannot operate without a particular order – or in her terms hegemony – it puts Mouffe more on the side of those who see democratic politics as 'archic' rather than 'anarchic.' Democratic politics cannot be executed without some order or stability.

One author whose views about democratic politics veer more towards the anarchic end of the spectrum is Jacques Rancière. In his work on democratic politics (for example, Rancière, 1995a; 1999; 2003; see also Bingham & Biesta, 2010) Rancière makes a distinction between two concepts: *police* (or police order) and *politics*. He defines 'police' as "an order of bodies that defines the allocation of ways of doing, ways of being, and ways of saying, and that sees that those bodies are assigned by name to a particular place and task" (Rancière, 1999, p. 29). It as an order "of the visible and the sayable that sees that a particular activity is visible and another is not, that this speech is understood as discourse and another as noise" (ibid.). Police should not be understood as the way in which the state structures the life of society because "(t)he distribution of places and roles that defines a police regime stems as much from the assumed spontaneity of social relations as from the rigidity of state functions" (ibid.). 'Policing' is therefore not so much about "the 'disciplining' of bodies" as it is "a rule governing their appearing, a configuration of *occupations* and the properties of the spaces where these occupations are distributed." (ibid.; emphasis in original). One way to read this definition of police is to think of it as an order that is *all-inclusive* in that everyone has a particular place, role, position or identity in it. This is not to say that everyone is included in the running of the order. The point simply is that no one is excluded from the order. After all, women, children, slaves and immigrants had a clear place in the democracy of Athens as those who were *not* allowed to participate in political decision-making. In precisely this respect every police order is all-inclusive (see also Biesta, 2009).

'Politics,' for Rancière, refers to "the mode of acting that perturbs this arrangement" (Rancière, 2003, p. 226) and that does so – and this is very important for getting the gist of Rancière's argument – with reference to the idea of *equality*. Politics therefore refers to "an extremely determined activity antagonistic to policing: whatever breaks with the tangible configuration whereby parties and parts or lack of them are defined by a presupposition that, by definition, has no place in that configuration" (ibid., pp. 29–30). This break is manifest is a series of actions "that reconfigure the space where parties, parts, or lack of parts have been defined" (ibid., p. 30). Political activity so conceived is therefore about "whatever shifts a body from the place assigned to it" (ibid.). "It makes visible what had no business being seen, and makes heard a discourse where once there was only place for noise." (ibid.) Politics thus refers to the event when two 'heterogeneous processes' meet: the police process and the process of *equality* (see ibid.). For Rancière politics understood in this way is always and necessarily *democratic* politics. He explicitly denies, however, that democracy can ever be "a regime or a social way of life" (ibid., p. 101). Democracy is not and cannot be part of the police order, but should rather be understood "as the institution of politics itself" (ibid., p. 101). Every politics is democratic *not* in the sense of a set of institutions, but in the sense of forms of expression "that confront the logic of equality with the logic of the police order" (ibid.). Democracy, so we might say, is a 'claim' for equality.

Whereas Rancière and Mouffe are therefore in agreement about the political significance of those moments at which an existing order is interrupted with reference to or in the name of the idea of equality, they differ in their outlook about whether the political is *only* located in the moment of interruption (Rancière) or whether the order that is established as a result of this is itself politically significant too (Mouffe). For Rancière the community that 'bears' the political is without any stable form and in that sense it is anarchic – that is, it is without form or structure – whereas for Mouffe the democratic community can have a stable form as long as it is not forgotten that this form is constituted hegemonically rather than on the basis of neutral or natural values and identities. However, what both deny – and this is the crucial point for my discussion – is that the political dimension of democratic politics can be completely 'covered' or captured by a particular order. Rancière would say that it can *never* be captured as an order, which implies that citizenship can no longer be thought of as a positive and stable identity. Mouffe would say that if we only focus on the democratic order and forget the political 'work' done in the establishment and maintenance of that order, we miss an important – and perhaps even the most important – aspect of democratic politics, which again implies that also for Mouffe citizenship ultimately can not be understood as only a stable and positive identity obtained through identification with an existing socio-political order.

THE BORDERS OF THE POLITICAL ORDER

The question as to how we might capture the 'essence' of democratic politics not only has to do with how we understand the location of democratic politics but is also related to how we understand the status of the borders of the democratic order – an issue which, to a large extent, is the corollary of the previous discussion. I have argued that at least some conceptions of liberal democracy would see the borders of the democratic order as circumscribing the domain of rationality and morality. Those who are on the inside, so the argument goes, are there because they are committed to act in a rational and moral way, while those on the outside of this order are there either because they are unable to act rationally and/or morally – and this inability can either be seen as structural or, as in the case of children, as temporal – or because they explicitly reject the standards of rationality and morality that characterise the political order. In strong versions of liberal democracy the borders are seen as natural and thus as uncontested and incontestable; in weaker – or more political – versions of liberal democracy the borders are understood as themselves political.

Seen from this angle, Mouffe stays rather close to this more political approach to liberalism. As I have shown, Mouffe does not deny that democratic politics needs order; her main concern is about the way in which we understand and represent this order and the processes through which the borders around this order are established. Mouffe does not advocate "pluralism without any frontiers" because she does not believe "that a democratic pluralist politics should consider as legitimate *all* the demands formulated in a given society" (Mouffe, 2005, p. 120; emphasis added). She argues that a democratic society "cannot treat those who put its basic institutions into question as legitimate adversaries" – but emphasises that exclusions should be envisaged "in political and not in moral terms" (ibid.). This means that when some demands are excluded, it is not because they are evil, "but because they challenge the institutions constitutive of the democratic political association" (ibid., p. 121). However – and this 'however' is crucial – for Mouffe "the very nature of those institutions" is also part of the debate. This is what she has in mind with her idea of a 'conflictual consensus' – which she describes as a "consensus on the ethico-political values of liberty and equality for all, [but] dissent about their interpretation" (ibid.). "A line should therefore be drawn between those who reject those values outright and those who, while accepting them, fight for conflicting interpretations." (ibid.) All this implies that for Mouffe "our allegiance to democratic values and institutions is not based on their superior rationality" which means that liberal democratic principles "can be defended only as being constitutive of our form of life" (ibid.) They are not the expression of a universal morality but are thoroughly 'ethico-political' (ibid.).

With regard to the question of borders and bordering this brings Mouffe's position closer to that of Rancière who, however, would argue that democracy *only* occurs in the redrawing of the borders of the police order and only when this redrawing is done with reference to equality. This is why Rancière holds that democracy is necessarily and essentially *sporadic*, that is, as something that only 'happens' from time to time and in very particular situations (see Rancière, 1995a, p. 41; p. 61; see also Biesta, 2009). This not only implies, as I have shown, that the 'essence' of politics cannot be captured if we only look at what happens within a particular order. It also means that there is a need to account for the work that happens at the borders of the democratic order including, if we follow Rancière, the work that happens at the very moment at which orders are being redrawn in the name of equality – if, that is, we wish to have a conception of citizenship that is sensitive to the political significance of these dimensions. (I will return to this below.)

DEMOCRATIC PROCESSES AND PRACTICES

In order to grasp the different dimensions of the political in democratic processes and practices, it is not only important to focus on how political communities are established and how borders are being drawn around them; there are also important questions about the processes and practices of democracy themselves. Whereas democracy is often understood in purely quantitative terms – an idea expressed in the notion of democracy as majority rule – an increasing number of political theorists have, over the past two decades, argued that democracy should not be confined to the simple aggregation of preferences but should involve the *deliberative trans-formation* of preferences. Under the deliberative model democratic decision-making is seen as a process which involves "decision making by means of arguments offered *by* and *to* participants" (Elster, 1998, p. 8) about the means *and* the ends of collective action. As Young explains, deliberative democracy is not about "determining what preferences have greatest numerical support, but [about] determining which proposals the collective agrees are supported by the best reasons" (Young, 2000, p. 23). The reference to 'best reasons' indicates that deliberative democracy is based upon a particular conception of deliberation. Dryzek, for example, acknowledges that deliberation can cover a rather broad spectrum of activities but argues that for *authentic* deliberation to happen the requirement is that the reflection on preferences should take place in a *non-coercive* manner (Dryzek, 2000, p. 2). This requirement, so he explains, "rules out domination via the exercise of power, manipulation, indoctrination, propaganda, deception, expression of mere self-interest, threats ... and attempts to impose ideological conformity" (ibid.). This resonates with Elster's claim that deliberative democracy is about the giving and taking of arguments by participants "who are committed to the values of rationality and impartiality"

(Elster, 1998, p. 8) and with his suggestion that deliberation must take place between "free, equal and rational agents" (ibid., p. 5).

The important thing about the deliberative turn is that it moves away from a mere arithmetical model of democracy – one that in the literature is known as the aggregative model – towards one that acknowledges that democracy is never simply about the aggregation of individual preferences but needs to engage with questions about the collective interest and the common good. From that angle democracy always requires the *translation* and *transformation* of private troubles into public issues, which, as I have shown in previous chapters, can be seen as one of the key functions of the public sphere. A limitation of some of the work within deliberative democracy is that it stays within a framework in which it is assumed that deliberation is only open for those who meet certain entry conditions – in the formulation of Elster these are the values of rationality and impartiality. This also assumes – as I will discuss in more detail below – that the political/civic identities of those who take part in the deliberation are already shaped *before* the deliberation starts.

This is also a point emphasised by Chantal Mouffe when she criticises deliberative democracy for its ambition to see power as a disturbing factor in democratic politics that needs to be overcome and ideally eliminated. The idea that democratic politics is about "the free and unconstrained public deliberation of all on matters of common concern" (Benhabib, quoted in Mouffe, 2000, p. 10) is mistaken, according to Mouffe, because relations of power are *constitutive* of the social (ibid., p. 14). The question for democracy, therefore, "is not how to eliminate power but how to constitute forms of power more compatible with democratic values" (ibid.). Mouffe presents her 'agonistic pluralism' as an alternative for deliberative democracy. Agonistic pluralism is based on a distinction between *the political*, by which Mouffe refers "to the dimension of antagonism that is inherent in human relations" (ibid., p. 15), and *politics*, by which she refers to "the ensemble of practices, discourses and institutions which seek to establish a certain order and organize human coexistence in conditions that are always potentially conflictual because they are affected by the dimension of 'the political'" (ibid.). For Mouffe politics, as I have shown above, thus aims at the creation "of a unity in a context of conflict and diversity" (ibid.). This always entails the creation of a distinction between 'us' and 'them.' Mouffe argues, however, that the "novelty of democratic politics is not the overcoming of this us/them opposition – which is an impossibility – but the different way in which it is established." (ibid.)

Mouffe's central insight here is for the need to transform antagonism into agonism, so that the 'them' in democratic politics is no longer perceived and approached as an enemy to be destructed, but as an adversary. Mouffe defines an adversary as a "legitimate enemy, one with whom we have some common ground because we have a shared adhesion to the ethico-political principles of liberal democracy: liberty and equality" but with whom "we disagree on the meaning and interpretation of those principles" (ibid.). While antagonism is the struggle between enemies, agonism refers to the struggle between adversaries, which is why Mouffe concludes that "from the perspective of 'agonistic pluralism' the aim of democratic politics is to transform *antagonism* into *agonism*" (ibid., p. 16; emphasis in original).

If my reading of Mouffe's work is correct, then I believe that the task of trans-formation is not only at stake in the *construction* of a particular political order – or in Mouffe's terms: the construction of politics – but is also an important element of the *modus operandi* of political orders so constructed. It is not as if all problems disappear as soon as a particular democratic hegemony is established. Questions about how to engage with conflict are likely to permeate democratic processes and practices, and the task of transforming antagonism into agonism so that we do not see our adversaries in moral terms of good versus bad but in political terms, that is, as pursuing a different *political* rather than *moral* agenda within a broader adhesion to the principles of liberty and equality, is an ongoing one.

Whereas for Mouffe there is democratic 'work' to be done *within* the domain of politics, that is, within a particular political order, Rancière's anarchic approach in a sense denies that anything politically relevant might happen within the police order. Or, to put it differently: for Rancière the 'essence' of democratic politics precisely occurs in the *interruption* of existing orders. This is why he holds that every politics is democratic *not* in the sense of a set of institutions, but in the sense of forms of expression "that confront the logic of equality with the logic of the police order" (Rancière, 2003, p. 101). Political activity is therefore always "a mode of expression that undoes the perceptible divisions of the police order by implementing a basically heterogeneous assumption, that of a part of those who have no part, an assumption that, at the end of the day, itself demonstrates the sheer contingency of the order [and] the equality of any speaking being with any other speaking being" (ibid., p. 30). This dispute, which Rancière identifies as the proper 'form' of democracy (for this expression see ibid., p. 225) – is not the opposition of interests or opinions between social parties. For Rancière democracy therefore is "neither the consultation of the various parties of society concerning their respective interests, nor the common law that imposes itself equally on everyone. The *demos* that gives it its name is neither the ideal people of sovereignty, nor the sum of the parties of society, nor even the poor and suffering sector of this society." (ibid.) The political dispute rather is a conflict "over the very count of those parties." (Rancière, 1999, p. 100) It is a dispute between "the police logic of the distribution of places and the political logic of the egalitarian act" (ibid.).

This is why Rancière argues that politics is "primarily a conflict over the existence of a common stage and over the existence and status of those present on it" (ibid., pp. 26–27). This is why the 'essence' of democracy/politics for Rancière is not a matter of consensus but of what he refers to as *dissensus* (see Rancière, 2003, p. 226; see also Rancière, 1999, pp. 95–121). But dissensus has a very precise meaning in Rancière's work. It is not the "opposition of interests or opinions (…), but the production, within a determined, sensible world, of a given that is heterogeneous to it" (Rancière, 2003, p. 226). This, then, is the democratic 'work' that emerges from Rancière's attempt to articulate the 'essence' of the political. While it might be tempting to say that this work occurs 'outside' of the existing police order, this 'outside,' in Rancière's thinking, does not denote the location of those who are excluded – after all, as I have argued above, for Rancière everyone is in a sense always included in any police order. It is rather an 'outside' that denotes a way of acting and being that cannot be conceived within the particular police order and in that way does not yet exist as a possible identity or way of being and speaking. This, however, raises an important question in relation to the fourth issue I wish to discuss. This is the question as to who the actor of democratic politics actually is.

THE SUBJECT OF POLITICS

As I have suggested above, liberal views about politics and the political community start from the assumption that political identities are formed and have to be formed *before* the 'event' of democratic politics. The reason for this stems from the fact that in order for democratic politics to occur – for example in the form of democratic deliberation – those who wish to take part in the process need to meet certain entry conditions such as, in the case of Elster's version of deliberative democracy, a commitment to the values of rationality and impartiality. This explains the particular role of education in the liberal view of democratic politics – and perhaps we might even say the *need* for education in the liberal view of democratic politics, in that education gets the task of making 'newcomers' ready for participation in democratic deliberation and decision-making. Education thus becomes a process of socialisation through which 'newcomers' become part and are inserted into the existing social and political order. Education is, in other words, the process that makes newcomers 'ready' for democracy on the assumption that democracy is only possible given this particular readiness of those who are assumed to take part.

Rancière's ideas about democratic politics are located at the other end of the spectrum in that for him democratic politics is precisely *not* about "the opposition of interests or opinions between social parties" (Rancière, 2003, p. 225); it is precisely *not* "the consultation of the various parties of society concerning their respective interests" (ibid.). For Rancière, therefore, democratic politics is not dependent upon the availability of a particular kind of political subjectivity but rather *generates* new political subjectivities. This is why Rancière emphasises that a political subject "is not a group that 'becomes aware' of itself, finds its voice, imposes its weight on society" (Rancière, 1999, p. 40), because establishing oneself as a subject does not happen before the 'act' of politics but rather in and through it. Rancière thus characterises a political subject as "an operator that connects and disconnects different areas, regions, identities, functions, and capacities existing in the configuration of a given experience – that is, in the nexus of distributions of the police order and whatever equality is already inscribed there, however, fragile and fleeting such inscriptions may be" (ibid.). Rancière gives the example of Jeanne Deroin who, in 1849, presented herself as a candidate for a legislative election in which she cannot run. Through this "she demonstrates the contradiction within a universal suffrage that excludes her sex from any such universality" (ibid., p. 41). It is the staging "of the very contradiction between police logic and political logic" that makes this into a political 'act' (ibid.), and it is in and through this act that political subjectivity is established.

For Rancière politics so conceived is a process of *subjectification* – a process in and through which political subjectivity is established and comes into existence or, to be more precise, a process through which *new* ways of doing and being come into existence. Subjectification here refers to "the production through a series of actions of a body and a capacity for enunciation not previously identifiable within a given field of experience, whose identification is thus part of the reconfiguration of the field of experience" (Rancière, 1999, p. 35; see also Rancière, 1995b). There are two things that are important in this definition, and they hang closely together. The first thing to emphasise is the supplementary 'nature' of subjectification (see Rancière, 2003, pp. 224–225). Subjectification, Rancière argues, is different from identification (see Rancière, 1995a, p. 37). Identification is about taking up an existing identity, that is, a way of being and speaking and of being identifiable and visible that is already possible within the existing order – or, to use Rancière's phrases, within the existing "perceptual field" or "sensible world" (Rancière, 2003, p. 226). Subjectification, on the other hand, is always "disidentification, removal from the naturalness of a place" (Rancière, 1995a, p. 36; see also Ruitenberg, 2010). Subjectification "inscribes a subject name as being different from any identified part of the community" (ibid., p. 37). When Rancière uses the notion of 'appearance' in this context, it is not, as he puts it, to refer to "the illusion masking the reality of reality" (Rancière, 2003, p. 224). Subjectification is about the appearance – the 'coming into presence,' as I have called it elsewhere (Biesta, 2006) – of a way of being that had no place and no part in the existing order of things. Subjectification is therefore a *supplement* to the existing order because it adds something to this order; and precisely for this reason the supplement also *divides* the existing order, that is, the existing "division of the sensible" (Rancière, 2003, pp. 224–225). Subjectification thus "redefines the field of experience that gave to each their identity with their lot" (Rancière, 1995a, p. 40). It "decomposes and recomposes the relationships between the ways of *doing*, of *being* and of *saying* that define the perceptible organization of the community" (ibid.; emphasis in original).

On this account, then, democratic politics does not require a particular kind of political subjectivity in order for it to be possible. The politic subject, the agent of democratic politics, arises in and with democratic action itself. In its shortest form: the political subject is not so much the producer of consensus as that it is the 'product' of dissensus. It is not, therefore, that education needs to make individuals ready for democratic politics; it is rather that through engagement in democratic politics political subjectivity is engendered. By turning the relationship between political subjectivity and democratic politics on its head, Rancière shifts education from its traditional place as the 'producer' of political subjectivities. This does not mean that there is no role at all to play for education but it is, as I will argue below, an entirely different one. Before I say more about these implications I want to turn briefly to the conception of political subjectivity in Mouffe's work.

Whereas Rancière's views about democratic politics are fundamentally anarchic so that there is no particular stable form for the subjectivity of the democratic citizen, and whereas the liberal approach to democratic politics is fundamentally 'archic' so that there is a clear template for the identity of the democratic person, Mouffe to some extent occupies a middle position between the two. As I have shown, what she shares with liberalism is the idea that politics in order to be possible needs to be 'archic,' it needs to have a certain form and continuity and stability, but Mouffe denies that this form is natural and also denies that there is only one possible form for democratic politics. The way in which the borders are being drawn and the 'arche' of politics is being constructed is a thoroughly political process and one that remains open for contestation albeit within the confines of "a shared adhesion to the ethico-political principles of liberal democracy" (Mouffe, 2000, p. 15).

One could say, therefore, that the kind of political subject 'needed' in Mouffe's political universe, is that of the person who is committed to the principles of liberty and equality and, more generally, to the political project of democracy. This is not only a more open kind of political subjectivity than what is assumed in (some) liberal conceptions of the political community in that Mouffe does not assume that there is only one valid definition of the principles of democratic politics. It is also a much more *political* kind of subjectivity in that democracy is not seen as a rational project, as something every rational being would ultimately opt for, but as a political and for that matter also a thoroughly historical 'project.' 'Commitment' is in this regard quite an appropriate term, because the kind of political subjectivity that Mouffe is hinting at is one that, to use her own words, is *passionate* about democracy. The aim of democratic politics, as we have seen, "is to transform *antagonism* into *agonism*" (ibid., p. 16). For Mouffe this requires "providing channels through which collective passions will be given ways to express themselves over issues, which, while allowing enough possibility for identification, will not construct the opponent as an enemy but as an adversary" (ibid.). This, in turn, means that "the prime task of democratic politics is not to eliminate passions from the sphere of the public, in order to render a rational consensus possible, but to mobile those passions towards democratic designs" (ibid.; see also Ruitenberg, 2009). The democratic subject, so we might say, is the one who is driven by a *desire* for democracy or, to be more precise, a desire for engagement with the ongoing experiment of democratic existence (for these terms see also Biesta, 2010[b]).

CONCLUSIONS: THE IGNORANT CITIZEN

In this chapter I have tried to argue that the 'essence' of democratic politics cannot be captured adequately if we think of democracy *only* as a stable political order. Although order is important for the everyday democratic conduct of our lives, we should not forget that any political order can only exist because of a division between 'inside' and 'outside.' With Mouffe I believe that this division is itself a crucial political event. To suggest that the border of the democratic order is natural, not only denies the political character of the division between inside and outside, but also forecloses the possibility to question how the borders are being drawn and therefore forecloses the possibility for a redrawing of the borders that might be able to expresses the values of liberty and equality in a more adequate manner. The redrawing of the borders of the political community is not just a quantitative matter – it is not a matter of bringing more individuals into a particular order; with Rancière I believe that the most significant re-drawings of the borders of the political order are those that are qualitative, that is, that generate new political identities and subjectivities. Here not only lies the importance of Rancière's more anarchic approach to democracy.

It is also a central element of his suggestion that democracy *is* a process of subjectification, a process in which new political identities and subjectivities come into existence.

Taken together these ideas form a significant departure from the conventional way in which education, citizenship and democracy are connected, because they challenge the idea that political subjectivities and identities *can be* and *have to be* fully formed before democracy can 'take off' – a way of thinking which I have characterised as a socialisation conception of civic learning and democratic education. The formation and ongoing transformation of political subjectivities rather *is* what democratic politics is about. The difference I have been trying to articulate in this chapter is therefore not between differing conceptions of what a good citizen is – in which case the underlying assumption that we can first decide what a good citizen is and then work on its 'production' through education and other means would remain uncontested – but between different ways in which we understand the relationships between citizenship, democracy and knowledge. I wish to refer to this 'other' citizen as the *ignorant citizen* in order to articulate that the democratic subject is not to be understood as a pre-defined identity that can simply be taught and learned, but has to be understood as emerging again and again in new and different ways through its very engagement with democratic processes and practices. The ignorant citizen is the one who is oblivious of the kind of 'good citizen' he or she is supposed to be. The ignorant citizen is the one who, in a sense, *refuses* this knowledge and, through this, refuses to be domesticated, refuses to be pinned down in a pre-determined civic identity. This does not mean that the ignorant citizen is completely 'out of order.' As I have tried to make clear in this chapter, the argument against an 'archic' understanding of democratic politics is not an argument for total anarchy; it is not an argument for saying that *any* interruption of the existing order is an instance of democracy. Rancière is very clear that dissensus is about the confrontation of the logic of the police order with the logic of *equality*, just as for Mouffe any redrawing of the existing political hegemony always needs to take place with reference to the principles of *liberty* and *equality*. The democratic project, in other words, is not without 'reference points' but it belongs to the very idea of democracy that these reference points engender a process that is fundamentally open and undetermined – which is why I have referred to democracy as an (ongoing) experiment. This is also why there is a need for a different conception of civic learning and democratic education, one in which civic learning is an inherent dimension of the ongoing experiment of democratic politics. Such a subjectification conception of civic learning is in many respects the opposite of a socialisation conception. Learning here is not about the acquisition of knowledge, skills, competencies or dispositions but has to do with an 'exposure' to and engagement with the experiment of democracy. It is this very engagement that is subjectifying. With Mouffe I believe that such an engagement is not based on a rational decision to become democratic – after all, in a very fundamental sense there is nothing rational about democracy – but is more driven by a desire for the particular mode of human togetherness that has developed over the centuries and to which the name 'democracy' has been given (see Biesta, 2010[b]). The desire for democracy does not operate at the level of cognition and therefore is not something that can simply be taught. The desire for democracy can, in a sense, only be fuelled. This is the reason why the most significant forms of civic learning are likely to take place through the processes and practices that make up the everyday lives of children, young people and adults and why the conditions that shape these processes and practices deserve our fullest attention if we really are concerned about the future of democratic citizenship and about the opportunities for democratic learning in school and society.

REFERENCES

Andrews, R., & Mycock, A. (2007). Citizenship education in the UK: Divergence within a multi-national State. *Citizenship Teaching and Learning, 3*(1), 73–88.

Aspin, D. N., & Chapman, J. D. (2001). Lifelong learning: Concepts, theories and values. In *Proceedings of the 31st Annual Conference of SCUTREA* (pp. 38–41). University of East London: SCUTREA.

Barnett, R. (1997). *Higher education: A critical business.* Buckingham: SRHE & Open University Press.

Batho, G. (1990). The history of the teaching of civics and citizenship in English schools. *The Curriculum Journal, 1*(1), 91–100.

Bauman, Z. (1999). *In search of politics.* Cambridge: Polity Press.

Bauman, Z. (2001). *Liquid modernity.* Cambridge: Polity Press.

Beck, J. (1998). *Morality and citizenship education in England.* London: Cassell.

Benn, R. (2000). The genesis of active citizenship in the learning society. *Studies in the Education of Adults, 32*(2), 241–256.

Biagioli, M. (Ed.). (1999). *The science studies reader.* New York: Routledge.

Biesta, G. J. J. (1992). *John Dewey: Theorie & praktijk.* Delft: Eburon.

Biesta, G. J. J. (1994). Education as practical intersubjectivity: Towards a critical-pragmatic understanding of education. *Educational Theory, 44*(3), 299–317.

Biesta, G. J. J. (2004[a]). Education, accountability and the ethical demand: Can the democratic potential of accountability be regained? *Educational Theory, 54*(3), 233–250.

Biesta, G. J. J. (2004[b]). "Mind the gap!" Communication and the educational relation. In C. Bingham & A. M. Sidorkin (Eds.), *No education without relation* (pp. 11–22). New York: Peter Lang.

Biesta, G. J. J. (2004[c]). The community of those who have nothing in common education and the language of responsibility. *Interchange, 35*(3), 307–324.

Biesta, G. J. J. (2006). *Beyond learning: Democratic education for a human future.* Boulder, CO: Paradigm Publishers.

Biesta, G. J. J. (2009). Sporadic democracy: Education, democracy and the question of inclusion. In M. Katz, S. Verducci & G. Biesta (Eds.), *Education, democracy and the moral life* (pp. 101–112). Dordrecht: Springer.

Biesta, G. J. J. (2010[a]). *Good education in an age of measurement: Ethics, politics, democracy.* Boulder, CO: Paradigm Publishers.

Biesta, G. J. J. (2010[b]). How to exist politically and learn from it: Hannah Arendt and the problem of democratic education. *Teachers College Record, 112*(2), 558–577.

Biesta, G. J. J., & Burbules, N. C. (2003). *Pragmatism and educational research.* Lanham, MD: Rowman and Littlefield.

Biesta, G. J. J., Lawy, R., & Kelly N. (2009). Understanding young people's citizenship learning in everyday life: The role of contexts, relationships and dispositions. *Education, Citizenship and Social Justice, 4*(1), 5–24.

Biesta, G. J. J., Stams, G. J. J. M., Dirks, E., Rutten, E. A., Veugelers, W., & Schuengel, C. (2001). Does sport make a difference? An exploration of the impact of sport on the social integration of young people. In J. Steenbergen, P. de Knop & A. H. F. Elling (Eds.), *Values and norms in sport* (pp. 95–113). Oxford: Meyer & Meyer Sport.

Bingham, C., & Biesta, G. J. J. with Jacques Rancière (2010). *Jacques Rancière: Education, truth, emancipation.* London/New York: Continuum.

Blee, H., & McClosky, A. (2003, September 17–20). *Perspectives on the provision of education for citizenship in Scotland and France, including a small-scale comparative study on pupil experience in Brittany and Scotland.* A paper presented at the European Conference on Educational Research, Hamburg. Retrieved from Education-line, August 18, 2008, from http://www.leeds.ac.uk/educol/ documents/oooo3495.html

REFERENCES

Bloomer, J. M. (1997). *Curriculum making in post-16 education: The social conditions of studentship.* London/New York: Routledge.
Bologna Declaration. (1999). *The European higher education area.* Joint declaration of the European Ministers of Education Convened in Bologna on the 19th June 1999.
Boshier, R. (1998). Edgard Faure after 25 years: Down but not out. In J. Holford, P. Jarvis & C. Griffin (Eds.), *International perspectives on lifelong learning* (pp. 3–20). London: Kogan Page.
Boshier, R. (2001). Lifelong learning as bungy jumping: In New Zealand what goes down doesn't always come up. *International Journal of Lifelong Education, 20*(5), 361–377.
Coare, P., & Johnston, R. (Eds.). (2003). *Adult learning, citizenship and community voices: Exploring community-based practice.* Leicester: Niace.
Crick, B. (1998). *Education for citizenship and the teaching of democracy in schools: Final report of the advisory group on citizenship.* London: QCA.
Crick, B. (2000). The English citizenship order: A temperate reply to critics. *The School Field, 11*(3/4), 61–72.
Crick, B. (2007). Citizenship: The political and the democratic. *British Journal of Educational Studies, 55*(3), 235–248.
Dawkins, R. (2006). *The God delusion.* London: Bantam Press.
Deakin Crick, R. (2008). Key competencies for education in a European context: Narratives of accountability or care. *European Educational Research Journal, 7*(3), 311–318.
Delanty, G. (2001). *Challenge knowledge: The University in the knowledge society.* Buckingham: Open University Press.
Delanty, G. (2003). Ideologies of the knowledge society and the cultural contradictions of higher education. *Policy Futures in Education, 1*(1), 71–82.
Dewey, J. (1916). Democracy and education. In J.-A. Boydston (Ed.), *John Dewey. The middle works (1899–1924)* (Vol. 9). Carbondale, IL: Southern Illinois University Press.
Dewey, J. (1925). Experience and nature. In J.-A. Boydston (Ed.), *John Dewey. The later works (1925–1953)* (Vol. 1). Carbondale, IL: Southern Illinois University Press.
Dewey, J. (1929). The quest for certainty. In J.-A. Boydston (Ed.), *John Dewey. The later works (1925–1953)* (Vol. 4). Carbondale, IL: Southern Illinois University Press.
Dewey, J. (1938[a]). *Experience and education.* New York: Macmillan.
Dewey, J. (1938[b]). Logic: The theory of inquiry. In J.-A. Boydston (Ed.), *John Dewey. The later works (1925–1953)* (Vol. 12). Carbondale, IL: Southern Illinois University Press.
Dewey, J. (1939). Experience, knowledge, and value: A rejoinder. In J.-A. Boydston (Ed.), *John Dewey. The later works (1925–1953)* (Vol. 14, pp. 3–90). Carbondale, IL: Southern Illinois University Press.
Dryzek, J. (2000). *Deliberative democracy and beyond: Liberals, critics, contestations.* Oxford: Oxford University Press.
Education Council. (2002, June 14). *Detailed work programme on the follow-up of the objectives of education and training systems in Europe.* Brussels: Author.
Edwards, R. (1997). *Changing places: Flexibility, lifelong learning, and a learning society.* London/New York: Routledge.
Elsdon, K. (1997). Voluntary organisations and communities: A critique and suggestions. In A. Bron, J. Field & E. Kurantowicz (Eds.), *Adult education and democratic citizenship II.* Krakow: Impuls.
Elster, J. (Ed.). (1998). *Deliberative democracy.* Cambridge: Cambridge University Press.
EUA. (2002). *Universities as the motor for the construction of a Europe of knowledge* (Input to the Barcelona summit). Brussels: Author.
EUA. (2003). *Response to the communication of the commission 'The role of the Universities in the Europe of knowledge.* Brussels: Author.
EUA. (2005). *Strong universities for a strong Europe.* Brussels: Author.
European Commission. (2008, June). *Eurobarometer 69. Public opinion in the European Union. First Results.*
European Commission. (2003, February). *The role of the universities in the Europe of knowledge.* COM (2003) 58, Brussels.

European Commission. (2005). *On the social agenda.* COM (2005) 33, Brussels.
European Commission. (2006). *Delivering on the modernization agenda for universities: Education, research and innovation.* COM (2006) 208, Brussels.
European Commission. (2000, January). *Towards a European research area.* COM (2000) 6, Brussels.
European Commission. (2001, November). *Making a European area of lifelong learning a reality.* COM (2001), 678, Brussels.
European Council. (2006). *Recommendations of the European Parliament and the Council of 18 December 2006 on key competencies for lifelong learning.* Brussels: Official Journal of the European Union.
Faulks, K. (1998). *Citizenship in modern Britain.* Edinburgh: Edinburgh University Press.
Faure, E., et al. (1972). *Learning to be: The world of education today and tomorrow.* Paris: UNESCO.
Fejes, A. (2004). New wine in old skins. Changing patterns in the governing of the adult learner in Sweden. *International Journal of Lifelong Education, 24*(1), 71–86.
Fernández, O. (2005). Towards European citizenship through higher education? *European Educational Research Journal, 40*(1), 59–68.
Field, J. (2000). *Lifelong learning and the new educational order.* Stoke-on-Trent: Trentham.
Fieldhouse, R. (1996). *A history of modern British adult education.* Leicester: NIACE.
France, A. (1998). 'Why should we care?' Young people, citizenship and questions of social responsibility. *Journal of Youth Studies, 1*(1), 97–111.
Fredriksson, U. (2003). Changes of education policies within the European Union in the light of globalisation. *European Educational Research Journal, 2*(4), 522–545.
Frenkel, S. (1999). *On the front line: Organization of work in the information economy.* Ithaca/London: ILR Press.
Fuller, S. (2003). Can Universities solve the problem of knowledge in society without succumbing to the knowledge society? *Policy Futures in Education, 1*(1), 106–124.
Garratt, D. (2000). Democratic citizenship in the curriculum: Some problems and possibilities. *Pedagogy, Culture and Society, 8*(3), 323–346.
Gellner, E. (1992). *Postmodernism, reason and religion.* London/New York: Routledge.
Gieryn, Th. F. (1983). Boundary-work and the demarcation of science from non-science: Strains and interests in professional ideologies of scientists. *American Sociological Review, 48*(December), 781–795.
Gilmour, I. (1992). *Dancing with dogma: Britain under Thatcherism.* London: Simon & Schuster.
Giroux, H. A. (2003). Selling out higher education. *Policy Futures in Education, 1*(1), 179–200.
Goodson, I. F., Biesta, G. J. J., Tedder, M., & Adair, N. (2010). *Narrative learning.* London/New York: Routledge.
Grace, A. P. (2004). Lifelong learning as a chameleonic concept and versatile practice: Y2K perspectives and trends. *International Journal of Lifelong Education, 23*(4), 385–405.
Hall, T., Williamson, H., & Coffey, A. (2000). Young people, citizenship and the third way: A role for the youth service? *Journal of Youth Studies, 3*(4), 461–472.
Haverhals, B. (2007). The normative foundations of research-based education: Philosophical notes on the transformation of the modern University idea. *Studies in Philosophy and Education, 26*(5), 419–432.
HMIE. (2003). *How good is our school? Education for citizenship.* Edinburgh: Author.
HMIE. (2006[a]). *Education for citizenship: A portrait of current practice in Scottish schools and pre-school centres.* Edinburgh: Author.
HMIE. (2006[b]). *Citizenship in Scotland's colleges. A report by HM Inspectorate of Education for the Scottish Further and Higher Education Funding Council.* Edinburgh: Author.
Holford, J. (2008). Hard measures for soft stuff: Citizenship indicators and educational policy under the Lisbon Strategy. *European Educational Research Journal, 7*(3), 331–343.
Holtgrewe, U., Kerst, Ch., & Shire, K. A. (Eds.). (2002). *Re-organizing service work: Call centres in Germany and Britain.* Aldershot: Ashgate.
Honig, B. (1993). *Political theory and the displacement of politics.* Ithaca, NY: Cornell University Press.
Horkheimer, M. (1947). *Eclipse of reason.* New York: Oxford University Press.
Hoskins, B. (2006). *A framework for the creation of indicators on active citizenship and education and training for active citizenship.* Ispra: Joint Research Centre.

REFERENCES

Hoskins, B. (2008). The discourse of social justice within European education policy: The example of key competencies and indicator development towards assuring the continuation of democracy. *European Educational Research Journal*, 7(3), 319–330.

Hoskins, B., D'Hombres, B., & Campbell, J. (2008). Does formal education have an impact on active citizenship behaviour? *European Educational Research Journal*, 7(3), 386–402.

Hoskins, B., Jesinghaus, J., Mascherini, M., *et al.* (2006). *Measuring active citizenship in Europe*. Ispra: European Commission Institute for the Protection and Security of the Citizen.

Hoskins, B., & Mascherini, M. (2009). Measuring active citizenship through the development of a composite indicator. *Journal of Social Indicators*, 90(3), 459–488.

Hoskins, B., Villalba, E., Van Nijlen, D., & Barber, C. (2008). *Measuring civic competence in Europe: A composite indicator based on IEA civic education study 1999 for 14 years old in School*. JRC Scientific and Technical Reports 23210 EN. Retrieved from http://ec.europa.eu/public_opinion/archives/eb/eb69/eb_69_first_en.pdf

Hutchins, R. M. (1936). *The higher learning in America*. New Haven, CT: Yale University Press.

Jarvis, P. (2000). 'Imprisoned in he global classroom' – revisited: Towards an ethical analysis of life-long learning. In *Proceedings of the first International Lifelong Learning Conference* (pp. 20–27). Rockhampton, Australia: Rockhampton University.

Katz, M., Verducci, S., & Biesta, G. (Eds.). (2009). *Education, democracy and the moral life*. Dordrecht/Boston: Springer Science + Business Media.

Kerr, D. (1999). Re-examining citizenship education in England. In J. Torney-Purta, J. Schwille & J.-A. Amadeo (Eds.), *Civic education across countries: Twenty- four case studies from the civic education project*. Amsterdam: IEA.

Kerr, D. (2000). Citizenship in the National Curriculum (England): Issues and challenges. *The School Field*, 11(3/4), 73–90.

Larsson, S. (2001). Study circles as democratic Utopia: A Swedish perspective. In A. Bron & M. Schemmann (Eds.), *Civil society, citizenship and learning*. Bochum: BSIAE.

Latour, B. (1983). Give me a laboratory and I will raise the world. In K. D. Knorr & M. Mulkay (Eds.), *Science observed* (pp. 141–170). London: Sage.

Latour, B. (1987). *Science in action*. Milton Keynes: Open University Press.

Latour, B. (1988). *The pasteurization of France*. Cambridge, MA: Harvard University Press.

Lawy, R. S., & Biesta, G. J. J. (2006). Citizenship-as-practice: The educational implications of an inclusive and relational understanding of citizenship. *British Journal of Educational Studies*, 54(1), 34–50.

Lindeman, E. (1926). *The meaning of adult education*. New York: New Republic.

Lisbon European Council. (2000, March 23–24). *Presidency conclusions*. Lisbon.

London Communiqué. (2007, May 18). *Towards the European higher education area*. London.

LTS (Learning and Teaching Scotland). (2000). *Education for citizenship: A paper for discussion and consultation*. Dundee: Author.

Mann, J. (1987). Ruling class strategies and citizenship. *Sociology*, 21(3), 339–354.

Mannion, G. (2003). Children's participation in school grounds developments: Creating a place for education that promotes children's social inclusion. *International Journal of Inclusive Education*, 7(2), 175–192.

Marquand, D. (2004). *Decline of the public: The hollowing-out of citizenship*. Cambridge: Policy Press.

Marshall, T. H. (1950). *Citizenship and social class and other essays*. Cambridge: Cambridge University Press.

Marshall, T. H. (1981). *The right to welfare and other essays*. London: Heinemann.

Martin, I. (2002). Adult education, lifelong learning and citizenship: Some ifs and buts. *International Journal of Lifelong Education*, 22(6), 566–579.

Martin, J., & Vincent, C. (1999). Parental voice: An exploration. *International Studies in Sociology of Education*, 9(3), 231–252.

McLaughlin, T. H. (2000). Citizenship education in England: The Crick report and beyond. *Journal of Philosophy of Education*, 34(4), 541–570.

Merrifield, J. (1997). Finding our lodestone again: Democracy, the civil society and adult education. In P. Armstrong, N. Miller & M. Zukas (Eds.), *Crossing borders, breaking boundaries*. London: University of London.

Mouffe, C. (1993). *The return of the political*. London/New York: Verso.

Mouffe, C. (2000). *Deliberative democracy and agonistic pluralism. Political Science Series 72*. Vienna: Institute for Advanced Studies.

Mouffe, C. (2005). *On the political*. London/New York: Routledge.

OECD. (1997). *Lifelong learning for all*. Paris: OECD.

Oelkers, J. (2005). Pragmatismus und Pädagogik: Zur Geschichte der Demokratischen Erziehungstheorie. In F. Busch & H.-J. Wätjen (Eds.), *Erziehen – Lehren – Lernen. Zu Kontinuitäten, Brüchen und Neuorientierungen im Pädagogischen Denken* (pp. 7–50). Oldenburg: Oldenburger Universitätsreden.

Oliver, J. E. (1999). The effects of metropolitan economic segregation on local civic participation. *American Journal of Political Science, 43*(1), 186–212.

Oliver, J. E. (2000). City size and civic involvement in metropolitan America. *American Political Science Review, 94*(2), 361–373.

Olssen, M. (1996). In defense of the welfare state and publicly provided education. *Journal of Education Policy, 11*(3), 337–362.

Osler, A., & Starkey, H. (2006). Education for democratic citizenship: A review of research, policy and practice 1995–2005. *Research Papers in Education, 21*(4), 433–466.

Pas, van der, N. (2001). Address by the European Commission. In *Adult lifelong learning in a Europe of knowledge. Conference report* (pp. 11–18). Sweden: Eskilstuna.

Pattie, C., Seyd, P., & Whiteley, P. (2004). *Citizenship in Britain: Values, participation and democracy*. Cambridge: Cambridge University Press.

Rancière, J. (1995a). *On the shores of politics*. London/New York: Verso.

Rancière, J. (1995b). Politics, identification, and subjectivization. In J. Rajchman (Ed.), *The identity in question* (pp. 63–70). New York/London: Routledge.

Rancière, J. (1999). *Dis-agreement: Politics and philosophy*. Minneapolis, MN: University of Minnesota Press.

Rancière, J. (2003). *The philosopher and his poor*. Durham, NC: Duke University Press.

Ranson, S. (Ed.), (1998). *Inside the learning society*. London: Cassell Education.

Rawls, J. (1996). *Political liberalism*. New York: Columbia University Press.

Roche, M. (1992). *Rethinking citizenship*. Cambridge: Polity Press.

Ross, H., & Munn, P. (2008). Representing self-in-society: Education for citizenship and the social-subjects curriculum in Scotland. *Journal of Curriculum Studies, 40*(2), 251–275.

Rowland, S. (2003). Teaching for democracy in higher education. *Teaching in Higher Education, 8*(1), 89–101.

Ruitenberg, C. (2009). Educating political adversaries. *Studies in Philosophy and Education, 28*(3), 269–281.

Ruitenberg, C. (2010). Queer politics in schools: A Rancièrean reading. *Educational Philosophy and Theory, 42*(5), 618–634.

Rychen, D. S. (2004). Key competencies for all: An overarching conceptual frame of reference. In D. S. Rychen & A. Tiana (Eds.), *Developing key competencies in education*. Geneva: UNESCO.

Sardar, Z. (2000). *Thomas Kuhn and the sciences wars*. London: Icon Books.

Schuller, T. (2001). The need for lifelong learning. In B. Crick (Ed.), *Citizens: Towards a citizenship culture*. Oxford: Blackwell Publishers.

Schuller, T., et al. (2004). *The benefits of learning: The impact of education on health, family life and social capital*. London: RoutledgeFalmer.

SE (Scottish Executive). (2004). *A curriculum for excellence*. Edinburgh: Scottish Executive.

Simons, M. (2006). 'Education through research' at European Universities: Notes on the orientation of academic research. *Journal of Philosophy of Education, 40*(1), 31–50.

Simons, M., Haverhals, B., & Biesta, G. (2007). Introduction: The University revisited. *Studies in Philosophy and Education, 26*(5), 395–405.

REFERENCES

Sleeper, R. W. (1986). *The necessity of pragmatism*. New Haven, CT: Yale University Press.
Trow, M. (1973). *Problems in the transition from elite to mass Higher Education*. Berkeley, CA: Carnegie Commission on Higher Education.
Vanderstraeten, R., & Biesta, G. J. J. (2001). How is education possible? *Educational Philosophy and Theory, 33*(1), 7–21.
Weerd, M. de, Gemmeke, M., Rigter, J. A. E., & Rij, C. van. (2005). *Indicators and options for monitoring active citizenship and citizenship education: Executive summary*. Amsterdam: Regioplan.
Westheimer, J., & Kahne, J. (2004). What kind of citizen? The politics of educating for democracy. *American Educational Research Journal, 41*(2), 237–269.
White, C., Bruce, S., & Ritchie, J. (2000). *Young people's politics: Political interest and engagement amongst 14- to 24-year olds*. York: YPS.
Wildermeersch, D., Stroobants, V., & Bron, M. (Eds.). (2005). *Active citizenship and multiple identities in Europe: A learning outlook*. Frankfurt am Main: Peter Lang.
Yeaxlee, B. A. (1929). *Lifelong education*. London: Cassell.
Young, I. M. (2000). *Inclusion and democracy*. Oxford: Oxford University Press.
Zgaga, P. (2007). *Higher Education in transition: Reconsiderations on Higher Education in Europe at the turn of the millennium. Monografier. Tidskrift för lärarutbildning och forskning*. Umeå: The Faculty Board for Teacher Education.